TEST SUCCESS

Targeting the
CTB-TerraNova

Reading and Language Arts • Mathematics

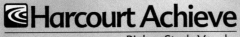

Harcourt Achieve

Rigby • Steck-Vaughn

www.HarcourtAchieve.com
1.800.531.5015

Harcourt Achieve Inc. is indebted to the following for permission to use material in this book:

page 32: Excerpts from "Island Dancer," reprinted with permission from *American Girl® Magazine*, January/February 1998 issue, text copyright © 1998 by Pleasant Company.

page 38: "Yo! Walk that Dog" by Barbara Kerley. Reprinted by permission of *CRICKET* magazine, January 1998, Vol. 25, No. 5, © 1998 by Barbara Kerley.

page 55: "The Ostrich Feather" from THE BUSHMEN AND THEIR STORIES by Elizabeth S. Helfman. Text copyright © 1971, renewed 1999 by Elizabeth S. Helfman. Reprinted by of permission Clarion Books/Houghton Mifflin Company. All rights reserved.

page 61: "The Priest's Towel" from *Many Lands, Many Stories* by David Conger published by Charles E. Tuttle Co. Reprinted by permission of Charles E. Tuttle Co., Inc. of Boston, Massachusetts and Tokyo, Japan.

Photo Credits:
p. 31 (tl) ©Myrleen Ferguson/PhotoEdit; p. 31 (tr) ©David Young-Wolf/PhotoEdit; p. 31 (b) ©Bonnie Kamin/PhotoEdit; p. 33 ©A. Ramey/PhotoEdit; p. 38 ©Tony Freeman/PhotoEdit.

The CTB and TerraNova tests are published by CTB McGraw-Hill.
Such company has neither endorsed nor authorized this test-preparation book.

ISBN: 0-7398-9753-5

4 5 6 7 8 9 2266 14
4500471747

Targeting the
CTB-TerraNova
Grade 5
CONTENTS

Dear Parent or Educator,

Welcome to **Targeting the CTB-TerraNova**. You have selected a book that will help your child develop the skills he or she needs to succeed on the CTB-TerraNova.

Although testing can be a source of anxiety for children, this book will give your child the preparation and practice that he or she needs to feel better prepared and more confident when taking the CTB-TerraNova. Research shows that children who are acquainted with the scoring format of standardized tests score higher on those tests. Students also score higher when they practice and understand the skills and objectives covered on the test.

This book has many features that will help you prepare your child to take the CTB-TerraNova:

- Lessons for the child about how to answer test questions and hints to guide the child toward the correct response
- Test-taking tips
- Tests that simulate the actual CTB-TerraNova tests
- A complete answer key

If your child expresses anxiety about taking a test or completing these lessons, help him or her understand what causes the stress. Then, talk about ways to eliminate anxiety. Above all, enjoy this time you spend with your child. He or she will feel your support, and test scores will improve as success in test taking is experienced.

Help your child maintain a positive attitude about taking a standardized test such as the CTB-TerraNova. Let your child know that each test provides an opportunity to shine.

Sincerely,

The Educators and Staff of
Harcourt School Supply

P.S. You might want to visit our website at www.HarcourtSchoolSupply.com for more test preparation materials as well as additional review of content areas.

Section
A

Reading and Language Arts

About Section A: Reading and Language Arts
This section of the book has been developed to refresh basic skills, familiarize your child with test formats and directions, and teach test-taking strategies. This section of the book is divided into three components: Lessons, Review Tests, and Comprehensive Test.

Lessons
There are lessons on reading comprehension and language arts skills assessed on the CTB-TerraNova Reading and Language Arts test. Each lesson contains:

- *Try This:* a skill strategy that enables your child to approach each lesson in a logical manner

- *Sample:* to familiarize your child with test-taking items

- *Think It Through:* the correct answer to the sample item and an explanation that tells why the correct answer is correct and why the incorrect answers are wrong

- several practice questions based on the lesson and modeled on the kinds of items found on the CTB-TerraNova

Review Test
The lessons are followed by a short Review Test that covers all the skills in the lessons. This test is designed to provide your child with independent practice that will familiarize him or her with the testing situation.

Comprehensive Test
The last component in this section is a Comprehensive Test. This test gives your child an opportunity to take a test under conditions that parallel those he or she will face when taking the CTB-TerraNova Reading and Language Arts test.

In order to simulate the CTB-TerraNova test as closely as possible, we have suggested time limits for the Comprehensive Test. This will enable your child to experience test taking under the same structured conditions that apply when achievement tests are administered. Furthermore, your child will have a final opportunity to apply the skills he or she has learned in this section prior to taking the CTB-TerraNova.

The recommended time limits are:
    Part 1: 40 minutes
    Part 2: 60 minutes

Have your child use the Reading and Language Arts Test Answer Sheet on page 109 to record the answers for this comprehensive test.

Answer Key
The Answer Key at the back of the book contains the answers for all the questions found in this section.

Reading

••••••• Lesson 1: Reading Comprehension

Directions: Read each passage carefully. Then read each question. Darken the circle for the correct answer.

Try This More than one answer may seem correct. Pick the best choice.

Sample A

Dancing

People the world over have danced through the ages. American Indians danced to celebrate the harvest. Africans danced to celebrate a successful hunt. Hawaiians used dance in place of a written language. And today, you dance just for fun.

This passage is mostly about

A different cultures

B reasons for dancing

C children's dances

D dancing in place of writing

Think It Through The correct answer is <u>B</u>, <u>reasons for dancing</u>. The story tells us the reasons people from different cultures dance.

Try This Read the question carefully. Then read all the choices.

Sample B

Stockton Street

Stockton Street is a story about a young girl growing up in San Francisco's Chinatown. Amy was interested in reading the story. She looked forward to learning about the place where her mother grew up.

Why did Amy want to read *Stockton Street*?

F Amy lived on Stockton Street.

G Amy's mother grew up in San Francisco's Chinatown.

H Chinatown was Amy's favorite place to visit.

J Amy liked mystery stories.

Think It Through The correct answer is G, <u>Amy's mother grew up in San Francisco's Chinatown</u>. The first sentence tells you that *Stockton Street* is about Chinatown in San Francisco. You also learn that Amy looked forward to learning about where her mother grew up. Amy wanted to read the book because her mother grew up in San Francisco's Chinatown.

Answers

SA Ⓐ Ⓑ Ⓒ Ⓓ

SB Ⓕ Ⓖ Ⓗ Ⓙ

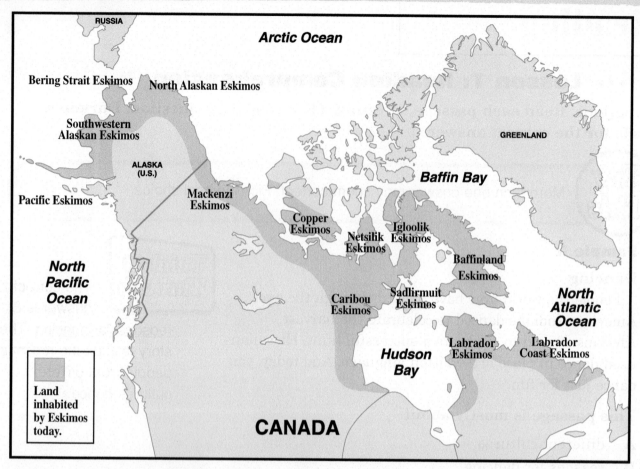

Directions: Read this passage about a game played by Canadian Eskimo children. Then read each question. Darken the circle for the correct answer.

Ajagag

A winter in the far northern part of the world lasts half a year. During those long, dark months, when the temperature goes down below freezing, children look for things to do. An old belief among the Canadian Inuit, or Eskimo, says that playing a game called *ajagag* makes the sun return faster in the spring.

If you ever get bored, try playing *ajagag*. It will help make the time go faster!

The object of *ajagag* is to catch a ring on a stick. Two or more people can play this game. You need a string about thirty inches long, a stick about seven inches long, and a curtain ring. Tie one end of the string to the stick. Tie the other end of the cord to the curtain ring. Now you are ready to play!

The first player holds the stick in one hand. Then she tosses the ring into the air with the other hand. She tries to catch the ring on the stick. One point is scored each time the ring is caught.

After each toss, the next player goes. After all players have gone ten times, add up the scores. The player with the most points wins the game.

1 In which drawing is someone playing ajagag?

A
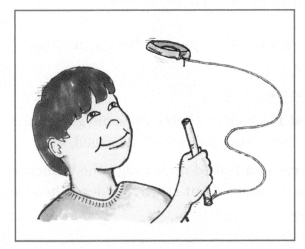

C

B
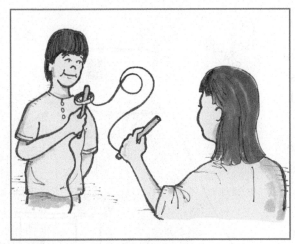

D

2 What is this passage mostly about?

F   games played in the winter

G   how to win *ajagag*

H   Canadian Eskimo children

J   a game called *ajagag*

3 Canadian Eskimo children look for things to do during the winter because they

A   don't know how to read

B   don't go to school

C   can't play outdoors

D   try to keep warm

4 If you did not have a curtain ring, what could you use instead?

F   a jar top

G   a bracelet

H   a picture frame

J   a finger ring

5 The <u>object</u> of *ajagag* is to catch a ring on a stick.

Another word for <u>object</u> is

A   meaning

B   end

C   purpose

D   thing

Fun in the Trees

"Lauren!" shouted Bennett. "Come see the tree house. I have something to show you."

"Did you get curtains?" teased Lauren.

Bennett laughed. "No, not yet. First I'm going to bring up some games and a sleeping bag so I can camp out at night. Now hurry up!" he urged.

Lauren trotted to the base of the tree and looked up through the branches of the ancient oak. Bennett led her up the uneven but sturdy ladder. When they reached the doorway to the tree house, Lauren stood up and looked around. Her eyes widened and she grinned at Bennett.

The first level of the tree house was large enough to fit a table and chairs for four. "Keep climbing," encouraged Bennett.

The second level was larger than the first. It contained a refrigerator box that was transformed into a sofa. "This looks like a great place to curl up with a good book," Lauren thought to herself.

"Next level," announced Bennett as he scrambled up the ladder.

When Lauren reached the third level, she knew immediately why Bennett was so excited about showing her the top of the tree house. His father had rigged an escape route from the third level. There was a large, long cable attached to the tree house. The cable angled down from the tree house until it reached the ground about fifty feet below. Attached to the cable was a handle on a track. Lauren grabbed the handle and transported herself down to the ground in a matter of seconds. Bennett used the pulley to retrieve the handle. He was quickly on the ground next to Lauren.

"Awesome!" exclaimed Lauren. "Your dad outdid himself this time!"

6 Why did Lauren's eyes widen when she stood up in the tree house?

    F The tree house was a disaster.

    G She was afraid she would fall from it.

    H She was amazed by the view.

    J She realized how much work went into it.

7 How big was the first level of the tree house?

    A just big enough for one person

    B the size of a refrigerator

    C big enough for a table with four chairs

    D as large as most kittens

8 What did Lauren want to do in the second level of the tree house?

    F read a book

    G camp out

    H put up curtains

    J play games

9 Why did Bennett take Lauren to the third level of the tree house?

    A to show her his new games

    B to let her see the bird's nest he had found there

    C so that she could help him make a sofa out of a refrigerator box

    D so that he could show her what his father had made

10 "Now hurry up!" Bennett <u>urged</u>.

The word <u>urged</u> means

    F insisted

    G cried

    H scolded

    J laughed

11 How did Lauren and Bennett get out of the tree house?

    A They climbed back down the ladder.

    B They jumped from the first level.

    C They rode the cable down to the ground.

    D They swung on a branch.

12 How did Lauren probably feel when she saw the escape route that Bennett's father had made?

    F excited

    G afraid

    H sorry

    J jealous

Directions: Read the story carefully. Then read the question. Darken the circle for the correct answer.

Sample

A Family Affair

Native Americans in the central part of the United States used their skill as horseback riders to hunt buffalo. The men would ride alongside a herd of animals and shoot them with bows and arrows. Women and children followed to skin the animals. The hides were used for tepees and clothing, and the meat was eaten.

What is this passage mostly about?

A bows and arrows

B family life

C hunting buffalo

D uses of buffalo hides

Directions: Here are two games that Chinese children play. Read about them. Then read each question. Darken the circle for the correct answer.

Game Time

The games children play in other countries have different names than the games children play here. However, they are often very similar to games we play.

In the game called Chinese Circle, a group of children form a circle. The circle is "closed" by everyone holding hands. Several children are picked to go inside the circle. Those making up the circle walk increasingly faster in one direction without letting go of each other's hands. The children in the center try to escape by darting between their friends' arms without touching anyone. The circle children don't try to prevent them from getting out. Instead, they try to help those escaping by slowing down the circle, dodging them, or raising their arms so the children can get through.

Dragon is a chain game that asks all the players to cooperate with one another. Ten children line up, one behind the other. Each puts his or her arms around the waist of the child in front. The first person in the line

represents the head of this long, twisty dragon. The last person in line is the tail. The head must catch the tail. All the other players must hang on to one another without breaking the chain. If the head catches the tail, they switch places and the game continues.

1 **Which is not part of the games you've read about?**

A The children walk faster and faster.

B The children in the circle try to escape.

C All the students must hang on to one another.

D The winner gets a prize.

2 **What is the lesson the players of Dragon learn?**

F The head catches the tail.

G The last child is always the dragon's tail.

H Players must cooperate with one another.

J Ten children line up, one behind the other.

3 **Where would be the best place to play these games at your school?**

A in the classroom

B in the hall

C in the gym

D in the cafeteria

4 **In Chinese Circle, the children in the center try to escape by _darting_ between their friends' arms.**

Another word for _darting_ is

F playing a game of darts

G circling around

H dashing

J walking

Directions: Here is a story that has a lesson. Read this story carefully. Then read each question. Darken the circle for the correct answer.

The Miller, his Son, and the Donkey

A miller and his son were driving their donkey to a nearby fair to sell him. They hadn't walked far when they passed a group of women gathered around a well. When one of the women saw the miller and his son she burst out laughing. "Have you ever seen such fools in your life?" she cried. "Just look at them. They're walking when they can ride!"

Gosh, thought the miller. *That's true. One of us can ride to the fair.*

"Nicholas," he said to his son. "Go on. Get up on the donkey. No sense in both of us dragging along like this." The boy happily agreed, and they set off again.

A mile down the road they came to a group of old men. The men were bent with age. "Ah ha!" cried one of the men, pointing a wrinkled finger at the miller and his son. "You see? Right there! That's exactly what I was talking about. Young people have no respect for their elders. Look at the way that boy is riding comfortably on that donkey while his old father has to walk."

That old guy has a point, thought the miller. *I should be the one riding to the fair, not this pip-squeak of a kid.*

"Off, Nicholas!" he shouted. "You've ridden long enough. Now it's my turn." The boy quickly climbed down, and they continued on their way.

Soon they passed several women and children who were picnicking by the side of the road. "Dear, dear, dear," said one of the women, shaking her head.

"That poor little boy. Look at him hurry along. He can barely keep up with the donkey's swift pace."

Gee, thought the miller when he heard the woman's remarks. *They must think I'm a terrible father!*

"Nicholas," he said, gently. "Come on, climb up and sit behind me. We'll both ride to the fair."

As they got near the fair, a man called to them. "Sir!" he cried. "Is that your donkey?" The miller nodded proudly, thinking that the man was interested in buying it.

"That's what I figured," said the man. "You certainly wouldn't abuse someone else's donkey. That's a fine animal," he added. "He no doubt serves you well. Is this the way you thank him, by loading all that weight onto his back? If you ask me, you ought to be carrying *him*!"

"Okay, okay," said the miller, anxious to please. "Nicholas, get off. Bend your back to the task. We shall carry our donkey the rest of the way." But the sight of a man and a little boy carrying a donkey was so ridiculous, everyone who saw it burst out laughing.

"Okay, that's it!" said the donkey. "Enough is enough. I will not be made fun of!" He began to kick and struggle in an attempt to break free.

"Pop! What's the donkey doing?" said Nicholas, losing his grip.

Getting away from the likes of you two, thought the donkey, and he trotted back across the bridge and disappeared among the wildflowers.

5 **What does the miller keep trying to do in this story?**

A sell his donkey

B please everybody

C avoid strangers

D instruct his son

6 **What did the miller do when the women at the well laughed at him?**

F He ignored them and continued on.

G He rode the donkey to the fair.

H He let his son ride the donkey.

J He warned them against laughing too loud.

7 **How does the miller feel when he overhears the picnicking women?**

A embarrassed

B angry

C confused

D gentle

8 **The man the miller met thought the miller was <u>abusing</u> his donkey.**

What does the word <u>abuse</u> mean?

F to laugh at

G to treat badly

H to struggle with something

J to be confused

9 **Which tells the main idea of this story?**

A Be careful what you wish for.

B If you try to please everyone, you will please no one.

C Know what you are going to do before you begin.

D Actions speak louder than words.

Directions: Here is a story about an American woman named Jane Addams. Read this story carefully. Then read each question. Darken the circle for the correct answer.

Jane Addams

"Mom, look over there! Isn't that Jane Addams?" asked Erich.

"Yes, yes, you are correct. That is Jane Addams. I would know her anywhere. She helped me settle into the American way of life when I first moved here from Germany," replied Ms. Schroeder.

"What do you mean, Mom?" asked Erich.

"When I first came to Chicago in 1890 I could not speak any English. I did not have a job. I did not know anyone either. I was only 19 years old, and I was determined to become an American citizen and become a successful person in the United States, but it was difficult. I heard about Jane Adda Hull House from another German immigrant. She told me that I could go to Hull House and learn English and get used to life in the United States," answered Ms. Schroeder.

"Did you go to Hull House, Mom?"

"I went as soon as I could get there. I signed up for an evening class to learn English. The social workers at Hull House were able to get me a job, too. It was not a great job. I stocked shelves at a small local grocery store, but it was a living. The social workers also helped me find a safe place to live. I shared a room in an apartment with two other women about my age. It worked out fine," said Ms. Schroeder.

"Did you ever talk to Jane Addams?" asked Erich.

"Jane Addams made it a point to talk to all the people who came to Hull House. After I finished my English classes, she asked to meet with me. She told me how I could become an American citizen. I took more classes at Hull House. This time I learned about the government of the United States. It was in this class that I met your father. He and I became American citizens in the same naturalization ceremony," explained Ms. Schroeder.

"Why did Jane Addams help establish Hull House? She knew how to speak English," asked Erich.

"She was a humanitarian. She saw a need for a community center that would help immigrants, young and old alike, find them homes and jobs, and help them become upstanding American citizens. She is my hero," stated Ms. Schroeder.

10 What is this passage mostly about?

   F Jane Addams and Hull House

   G the life of Erich Schroeder

   H the history of Chicago

   J immigrant life

11 Why did Ms. Schroeder come to the United States?

   A She wanted to search for gold.

   B She hoped to learn to speak English.

   C She wanted to find a job in a grocery store.

   D She wanted to become a citizen of the United States.

12 How did Ms. Schroeder find out about Hull House?

   F A German immigrant told her about it.

   G Ms. Schroeder heard about Hull House when she still lived in Germany.

   H She read a newspaper article about Hull House and Jane Addams.

   J Jane Addams invited her to come to Hull House.

13 What did Ms. Schroeder need to do in order to become a citizen of the United States?

   A She needed to find a safe place to live.

   B She needed to get married.

   C She had to have a well-paying job.

   D She had to learn about the government of the United States.

14 Ms. Schroeder did not think her first job in America was a great job, "but it was a living." What does that mean?

   F It was a life-long dream.

   G It was a way to make money.

   H It was a safe place to live.

   J It was too crowded to breathe.

15 Which word best describes Jane Addams?

   A heartless

   B controlling

   C rich

   D merciful

16 Your answer choice for question 15 is best supported by which idea from the story?

   F Jane Addams told Ms. Schroeder how to become an American citizen.

   G Jane Addams made it a point to talk to all the people who came to Hull House.

   H Jane Addams was a humanitarian.

   J Jane Addams knew how to speak English.

Language Arts

Directions: Read each sample. Darken the circle for the correct answer.

 Choose the sentence that best combines both sentences into one. Make sure the sentence you choose has the same meaning as the two separate sentences.

Sample A

American Indians were the only people who lived in America.
The settlers drove them off their land.

A American Indians, until the settlers drove them off their land, were the only people in America.

B American Indians were the only people who lived in America until the settlers drove them off their land.

C The settlers drove the American Indians, the only people who lived in America, off their land.

D American Indians were the only people who lived in America, the settlers drove them off their land.

 The correct answer is <u>B</u>, <u>American Indians were the only people who lived in America until the settlers drove them off their land.</u> This is the only choice in which the action is in order and the sentence has the proper punctuation.

 Choose the sentence that is written correctly. Think of the rules that you have learned, and pick the sentence that follows all the rules.

Sample B

F She dance very well.

G He can't dance very well.

H They dances very well.

J He dancing in the ballroom.

 The correct answer is <u>G</u>, <u>He can't dance very well.</u> The verb must agree with the subject. "She dance" and "They dances" do not agree. "Dancing" is not a verb that can stand on its own.

Answers
SA Ⓐ Ⓑ Ⓒ Ⓓ
18 SB Ⓕ Ⓖ Ⓗ Ⓙ

Directions: Choose the sentence that best combines both sentences into one.

1 *John grew up blind.*
   He was determined that his blindness would not hold him back.

   A John grew up blind, but he was determined that it would not hold him back.

   B Blindness, which John grew up with, did not hold him back.

   C John grew up with blindness that did not hold him back because of determination.

   D Determined that blindness would not hold him back, John grew up.

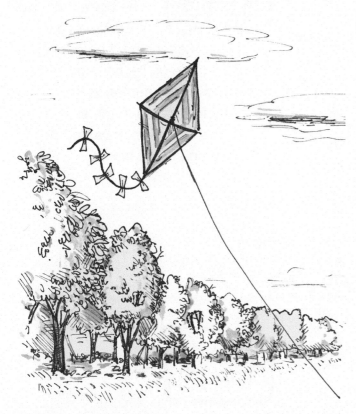

2 *That day we each made our own kites.*
   That day we also flew them in the park.

   F That day we flew the kites in the park that we each made.

   G Making our own kites, we flew them in the park that day.

   H That day we each made our own kites and flew them in the park.

   J We each made our own kites that day and flew them in the park that day.

Directions: Choose the sentence that is written correctly.

3 **A** American Indians are the first people who lived in the Americas.

   B Today, the tribes gather so them can renew their culture.

   C Dancing was an important part of today's powwows.

   D The drummer's beat signaling when to speed up the dance.

4 **F** The healers cure people they are called medicine men.

   G The ceremonies held by American Indians.

   H Tribal meetings help their people to better.

   J They enjoyed themselves at the powwow.

Answers

1 Ⓐ Ⓑ Ⓒ Ⓓ   3 Ⓐ Ⓑ Ⓒ Ⓓ
2 Ⓕ Ⓖ Ⓗ Ⓙ   4 Ⓕ Ⓖ Ⓗ Ⓙ

Directions: Read each sample. Darken the circle for the correct answer.

Choose the sentence that best completes the story. Try each answer in place of the missing sentence. Only one choice belongs. Pick the one that makes the most sense in the story.

Sample A

Angela has shown great talent in her sketches since she was young. She hopes some day to be a fashion designer. _____. After she graduates, she plans to work for a fashion house.

A Then she can put her talent to work.

B It has always been her dream.

C Her part-time job will help pay for college.

D Next year she's attending the Fashion Institute of Technology.

The correct answer is <u>D</u>, <u>Next year she's attending the Fashion Institute of Technology.</u> This is the only sentence that makes sense in the story. The other sentences do not complete the story.

Here is a topic sentence. Pick the sentences that best support it. Try reading each choice after the topic sentence.

Sample B

There are many famous people who have overcome physical handicaps to lead successful lives.

F People say the best basketball player of all time is Michael Jordan. It's amazing how many points he can score in a game.

G Franklin Delano Roosevelt was paralyzed from polio. However, he still became President of the United States.

H Tara Lapinski won the Olympic gold in figure skating. At 15 years old, she was the youngest woman to do this.

J Most people have to work hard to achieve what they want. But some people are lucky and end up in the right place at the right time.

The correct answer is <u>G</u>, <u>Franklin Delano Roosevelt was paralyzed from polio. However, he still became President of the United States.</u> These are the only sentences that explain the main idea of the story. The other choices are about famous people or achieving fame. But they are not examples of what is stated in the topic sentence.

Answers

SA Ⓐ Ⓑ Ⓒ ●

20 SB Ⓕ ● Ⓗ Ⓙ

Directions: Choose the sentence that best completes the story.

1   Publishing a magazine, like any other business, needs a lot of thought. First a publisher has to decide on the type of magazine she wants to publish. _____. Finally, she must put together the best staff of people she can find and try to make a go of it!

  A   Then she needs to make sure there will be people who will want to read it.

  B   Then she needs to make her magazine's cover bright and cheerful.

  C   Then she needs to interview as many people as necessary to find the right staff.

  D   Then she needs to write all the stories to go in it.

2   Earthquakes can be dangerous. Since they can't be stopped, we have to do what we can to predict them. _____. This will help us to save lives.

  F   Some animals begin to act strangely before an earthquake.

  G   If we know when they are coming, we can be prepared.

  H   Seismologists are scientists that study earthquakes.

  J   People in earthquake zones should move.

Directions: Choose the sentences that best support the topic sentence.

3   *The black bear, one of the largest mammals in the United States, was close to extinction by the early 1900s.*

  A   Adult bears are huge, but babies are tiny. They are usually born two at a time.

  B   Because of their great size, people feared the bears. They hunted them in great numbers.

  C   There is much to learn about these amazing animals. Today, luckily, they are here to stay.

  D   These bears can travel great distances in search of food. They are excellent climbers.

4   *There are so many dandelions that people often take them for granted.*

  F   These plants, however, were once so prized in Europe, they were transported to North America by the early settlers. Here they were used for food and medicine.

  G   After careful cleaning and sorting, the leaves can be boiled and eaten. Some people will eat the leaves raw in a salad.

  H   Any part of the dandelion root can create a new plant. If the flower is destroyed, the root will produce another plant.

  J   Few people plant dandelions today. They are never welcome on anyone's front lawn.

Answers

1 Ⓐ Ⓑ Ⓒ Ⓓ   3 Ⓐ Ⓑ Ⓒ Ⓓ

2 Ⓕ Ⓖ Ⓗ Ⓙ   4 Ⓕ Ⓖ Ⓗ Ⓙ

Directions: Read the draft. Darken the circle for the correct answer.

1. People have told stories throughout the ages. 2. Many of these stories attempt to explain either how to act or why things happen. 3. In the old days, most people couldn't read or write. 4. So it was easier to tell a story and pass it along from generation to generation. 5. Many people use computers today. 6. Of course, today most people can read. 7. But these old tales are still fun to hear.

 Choose the best way to rewrite sentence I. Remember, the best way to write it may be the way it appears in the story.

Sample A

A   People has told stories throughout the ages.

B   Throughout the ages, people has told stories.

C   Throughout the ages, people have telled stories.

D   It is best as it is.

 The correct answer is D, It is best as it is. The verbs in the other choices do not agree with their subjects.

 Pick the sentence that does not belong in the story. Look for the sentence that does not relate to the topic sentence.

Sample B

F   sentence 2

G   sentence 3

H   sentence 4

J   sentence 5

 The correct answer is J, sentence 5. If you take that sentence out of the passage, it will actually make the passage read better.

Answers
SA Ⓐ Ⓑ Ⓒ Ⓓ
22 SB Ⓕ Ⓖ Ⓗ Ⓙ

Directions: Read this draft of a letter. Then answer the questions that follow.

Dear Professor Frank:

1. Me and my friend enjoyed your talk very much. 2. We both very happy we came. 3. You told many good stories about animals. 4. We hoping to be like you some day.

Sincerely yours,
Leary

1   Choose the best way to write sentence 1.

A   My friend and me enjoyed your talk very much.

B   Us enjoyed your talk very much.

C   My friend and I enjoyed your talk very much.

D   It is best as it is.

2   Choose the best way to write sentence 2.

F   Both are very happy we came.

G   We am both very happy we came.

H   We are both very happy we came.

J   It is best as it is.

3   Choose the best way to write sentence 4.

A   We hopes to be like you someday.

B   We are hoping to be like you some day.

C   We is hoping to be like you some day.

D   It is best as it is.

Answers

1   Ⓐ Ⓑ Ⓒ Ⓓ   3   Ⓐ Ⓑ Ⓒ Ⓓ

2   Ⓕ Ⓖ Ⓗ Ⓙ

Directions: Choose the sentence that is written correctly. Darken the circle for the correct answer.

Sample

A We hasn't seen so much rain in a long time.

B The rain made many trees falled to earth.

C The rain rolled down the roof.

D The rain were falling.

Directions: Here is a report about insects. There are some mistakes in the report. Read it carefully, then read each question. Darken the circle for the correct answer.

Insects

1. Insects have a bad reputation we think of them as pests that bite or sting. 2. Some of them carry diseases, but they was helpful to nature. 3. Insects help plants and trees to grow and provide food for birds and animals. 4. They helps to make the world a cleaner place to live. 5. When I realized how important insects are. 6. The report took on a different tone. 7. One reason people dislike insects is there are so many of them, and we can't seem to control them. 8. The more we try to destroy them, the more they seem to thrive.

1 Choose the best way to write sentence 2.

A Some of them carry diseases, but they wasn't helpful to nature.

B Some of them carry diseases, but they are helpful to nature.

C Some of them carry diseases, but they is helpful to nature.

D It is best as it is.

2 Choose the best way to write sentence 4.

F They helped to make the world a cleaner place to live.

G They helping to make the world a cleaner place to live.

H They help to make the world a cleaner place to live.

J It is best as it is.

3 Choose the best way to combine sentences 5 and 6.

A When the report took on a different tone, I realized how important insects are.

B When I realized how important insects are and the report took on a different tone.

C When I realized how important insects are, the report took on a different tone.

D It is best as it is.

4 Choose the sentence that contains two complete thoughts and should be written as two sentences.

F sentence 1

G sentence 3

H sentence 5

J sentence 7

5 Choose where this sentence best fits in the paragraph.

I began to appreciate what insects do.

A after sentence 2

B after sentence 3

C after sentence 6

D after sentence 7

Directions: Here is a report about Duke Ellington, a famous musician. There are some mistakes in the report. Read it carefully, then read each question. Darken the circle for the correct answer.

Duke Ellington

1. Duke Ellington was one of America's greatest jazz composers. 2. He wrote his first piece when he was 14 years old. 3. He was a soda fountain clerk when he wrote his first piece. 4. It was called, "Soda Fountain Ragtime." 5. Many of his songs are classics. 6. He done wrote more than a thousand songs. 7. They included symphonies, jazz, and church music. 8. Beethoven also wrote music as a young boy.

6 **Choose the best way to combine sentences 2 and 3.**

F He wrote his first piece when he was 14 years old and a soda fountain clerk.

G He was a 14-year-old soda fountain clerk when he wrote his first piece.

H He was a soda fountain clerk for 14 years when he wrote his first piece.

J It is best as it is.

7 **Choose the best way to write sentence 6.**

A He wrote more than a thousand songs.

B He writed more than a thousand songs.

C He done writes more than a thousand song.

D It is best as it is.

8 **Choose the sentence that does <u>not</u> belong.**

F sentence 2

G sentence 4

H sentence 6

J sentence 8

Answers

6 Ⓕ Ⓖ Ⓗ Ⓙ   **8** Ⓕ Ⓖ Ⓗ Ⓙ

26 **7** Ⓐ Ⓑ Ⓒ Ⓓ

Directions: Here is the second paragraph of the report.

1. In 1918 Ellington formed a band that lasted for 56 years. 2. Although he played the piano, people said that his real instrument was his band. 3. He played soft music. 4. He played mellow tunes. 5. He played velvety melodies.

9 Choose the best way to combine sentences 3, 4, and 5.

A Playing music of soft, mellow tunes and velvety melodies.

B He played soft music with mellow tunes and velvety melodies.

C He played soft music also mellow tunes and also velvety melodies.

D To play music he picked soft, mellow tunes and velvety melodies.

10 Choose where this sentence best fits in the paragraph.

This type of music was called "The Ellington Effect."

F after sentence 1

G after sentence 2

H after sentence 3

J after sentence 5

Directions: Here is the third paragraph of the report.

1. He took his band to Europe there Ellington was treated like a true Duke. 2. France gave him its highest award, the Legion of Honor. 3. He also played before the Queen of England at request. 4. Later on when he was 70 years old, he was awarded the Presidential Medal of Freedom by President Nixon.

11 Choose the sentence that contains two complete thoughts and should be written as two sentences.

A sentence 1

B sentence 2

C sentence 3

D sentence 4

12 Choose the best way to write sentence 3.

F He also played before the Queen of England at she request.

G He also played before the Queen of England at the request.

H He also played before the Queen of England at her request.

J It is best as it is.

Answers

9 Ⓐ Ⓑ Ⓒ Ⓓ   11 Ⓐ Ⓑ Ⓒ Ⓓ

10 Ⓕ Ⓖ Ⓗ Ⓙ   12 Ⓕ Ⓖ Ⓗ Ⓙ

Directions: Here is a passage about animals. Read this passage. Then read each question. Darken the circle for the correct answer.

Animal Facts and Myths

People and animals have shared the earth since the beginning of time. Over the years some animals have acquired reputations as being vicious and dangerous, while others have been seen as friendly and harmless.

For instance, lions are imposing animals. But lions are not as dangerous as tigers or leopards. Lions tend to be relaxed and friendly unless they are hungry. Usually lions kill only for food and to keep the pride safe from intruders.

13 Choose the sentence that is written correctly.

A   Probably no animal has a worse reputation than the wolf.

B   Thought of as sly and vicious creatures.

C   Wolves raiding farms and killing livestock.

D   Today wolves were found only in small parts of the United States.

14 Choose the sentence that best completes the story.

Wolves love company and often live in packs. ____ . Males and females usually mate for life. Wolves are curious and often come near people. But scientists have not been able to find one proven case of a person being attacked by wolves in North America.

F   During the Middle Ages, there were many wolves, and they posed a threat to people.

G   This dislike was passed down through the generations.

H   The father helps care for the young cubs.

J   They have a very close family life.

15 Choose the sentences that best support the topic sentence.

In fairy tales, bears are often pictured as charming creatures.

A   The soft, cuddly look of cubs has also made the "teddy bear" a favorite stuffed animal. But if you were to meet a bear in the wilderness, you might not think it was so charming.

B   In the past, people sometimes caught bear cubs and took them home as pets. The cubs' curiosity made them easy to catch.

C   In the wild, both grizzly bears and black bears can be dangerous. They are suspicious of strangers and do not like to be startled or surprised.

D   Everyone loves *Goldilocks and the Three Bears*. In this tale, each bear is a different size.

Answers

13 Ⓐ Ⓑ Ⓒ Ⓓ   15 Ⓐ Ⓑ Ⓒ Ⓓ

28 14 Ⓕ Ⓖ Ⓗ Ⓙ

STOP

Directions: Read each sample. Darken the circle for the correct answer. Remember to use the answer sheet on page 109 to fill in your answers.

Sample A

Katrina is very excited about going camping with her cousins, Gary and Linda. The cousins are good friends. The campers plan to travel to the Grand Canyon where they will stay for two weeks.

On their trip the three cousins most likely will

A   be very bored

B   fight and argue

C   have an enjoyable time

D   not talk to one another

Go

Directions: Here is a report about elephants. There are some mistakes in the report. Read it carefully, then read each question. Darken the circle for the correct answer. Remember to use the answer sheet on page 109 to fill in your answers.

1. I find elephants very interesting. 2. Their trunk is so long that it weighs about 300 pounds. 3. They also use their trunk to hold things. 4. The trunk working almost like a hand.

Sample B

Choose the best way to write sentence 4.

F   The trunk works almost like a hand.

G   The trunk work almost like a hand.

H   The trunk worked almost like a hand.

J   It is best as it is.

Sample C

Choose where this sentence best fits in the paragraph.

Elephants use their trunk to smell.

A   after sentence 1

B   after sentence 2

C   after sentence 3

D   after sentence 4

Part 1

How Do You Have Fun?

Having fun is an important part of life. Since the earliest times, people have invented ways to enjoy themselves and at the same time exercise their bodies and minds. In this theme, you will read stories about recreational activities. You will probably get some new ideas about why people dance, play sports, and invent toys and games. You will see why having fun is more than just–fun!

Directions: In this selection by Therese K. Smith, you will read about 12-year-old Kehaulani DeRego. She is a Hawaiian girl who enjoys learning the traditional Hula dances of her people. Hula dances are older than the written language of the Hawaiian people and were once an important way of retelling the legends of the island. Read the story. Then answer each question.

Island Dancer

Kehaulani DeRego, 12, looks like a vision from long-ago Hawaii. Her fern skirt sways as she dips and steps in the moves of an ancient hula. As she dances, Kehaulani paints a picture with her hands, telling a story of her land and her ancestors.

More Than a Dance

"The hula is a dance designed to tell important stories, not just to entertain," explains Kehaulani (KAY-how-LAH-nee). The hula developed centuries ago, when Hawaiians had no written language. History and stories were passed by word of mouth or set to music and danced. A hula might pass on the legend of Laka, the goddess of dance. It might record events of the time, praise a Hawaiian queen, or describe the beauty of the islands.

"The stories talk about my ancestors and what happened before I was born," says Kehaulani. "It's a fun way to learn about history."

Kehaulani lives on the island of Oahu and has been dancing since she was two years old. Her family has been involved with hula for generations. Kehaulani's grandmother and great-grandmother both taught hula schools, or *halaus* (huh-LAOWZ). Kehaulani's mother is the teacher of her hula school, Halau Hula O'Hokulani.

In hula, your family includes more than blood relatives. Members of the hula school spend so much time practicing and performing together, they become a kind of family. Kehaulani calls the other adults "aunties" and "uncles." The dancers are her hula sisters and hula brothers.

Making Leis

Hula families do more than dance together. The dancers learn from adults how to make *leis* (layz), the garlands worn around the neck, head, wrists, and ankles.

Today a group of dancers and their fathers are preparing to gather ferns for making leis. Kehaulani listens carefully as her father explains that they are here not to take from the forest but to share its beauty with others. Then the fathers and daughters pair off and quietly enter the forest. They climb the steep hill and begin to snap fern branches off the plants.

When enough ferns are gathered, dancers are ready to make leis with their mothers and fathers. The youngest girls spray the ferns with water to keep them fresh. Others pull individual branches off each stem and hand them to a partner to braid.

Celebrating Hula

Kehaulani is surrounded by dancers onstage at a hula festival, one of the many events where the halau performs through the year. She is radiant in her long dress, called a *mu'u mu'u* (MOO-oo MOO-oo). Around her neck is a lei of polished nuts. More than 20 delicate plumeria flowers have been tucked, one by one, around her braided bun.

"When I dance, I think about the song and try to make people enjoy it as much as I do," explains Kehaulani. The dance she does on this day is called "Children of the Land." It tells of a young girl who listens carefully to her grandmother's stories—legends of a magical shell, a shark transformed into a man, and of Pele, the jealous goddess of the volcano.

"The song takes me on an adventure through different stories," says Kehaulani. It also teaches a lesson—that all of Hawaii's children should listen to the stories of long-ago days. As Kehaulani steps and turns in the dance her mother taught her, a beautiful story is passed on to the audience, and to future generations of hula sisters.

1 **This passage is mostly about**

    A   the Hawaiians' written language

    B   Laka, the goddess of dance

    C   a dance that tells a story

    D   going to hula school

2 **Kehaulani feels the hula dance is a**

    F   way to entertain her relatives

    G   fun way to learn about history

    H   way to spend more time with her family

    J   a chore she does not like to do

3 **Which fact from the story helped you to answer question 2?**

    A   In hula, your family includes more than blood relatives.

    B   Kehaulani has been dancing since she was two years old.

    C   The hula was developed centuries ago.

    D   The stories tell about ancestors and events before Kehaulani was born.

4 **Which statement best shows why the hula dancers are a family?**

    F   In hula, your family includes more than blood relatives.

    G   The dancers are Kehaulani's hula sisters and hula brothers.

    H   Kehaulani calls the adults auntie and uncle.

    J   The dancers spend so much time practicing and performing together.

5 **Which is an *opinion* stated in the passage?**

    A   In hula, your family includes more than blood relatives.

    B   She is radiant in her long dress, called a *mu'u mu'u*.

    C   The dance she does on this day is called "Children of the Land."

    D   Kenaulani is surrounded by dancers onstage at a hula festival.

6 **Why does Kehaulani's father tell the dancers that they are not there to take from the forest?**

    F   so they dance better

    G   so they use nuts instead of ferns for the leis

    H   so they only take what they need

    J   so they get their ferns somewhere else

7 Here is a time line of some events in the passage. What happens next?

| Kehaulani and her father enter the forest. | ⇨ | Fathers and daughters snap fern branches off the plants. | ⇨ | Ferns are sprayed with water. | ⇨ | ? |

   A   Kehaulani's father speaks about the forest.

   B   The girls gently pick the ferns.

   C   The fathers and daughters pair off.

   D   The ferns are braided.

8 Kehaulani is described as <u>radiant</u> in her long dress.

Used this way, the word <u>radiant</u> probably means

   F   beautiful

   G   powerful

   H   giving off energy

   J   pleased

9 What is something that the movements of the hula do <u>not</u> do?

   A   entertain visitors

   B   tell a story

   C   make a picture

   D   braid hair

Directions: After reading "Island Dancer," one of the students researched the art of dance and wrote about what she discovered. There are several mistakes in her work that need correcting. Read it carefully, then read each question. Darken the circle for the correct answer.

Dancing

1. Dancing are one of the oldest and liveliest of the arts. 2. There are pictures on cave walls that show primitive dance. 3. There are even ancient writings that tell why people dance. 4. Does dance do what for us? 5. It is the language of the body. 6. It bring people together in thought and feelings. 7. A dancer can get people to understand any subject or idea. 8. Her movements can tell about religious history. 9. Her movements can tell about everyday life. 10. Can use any style or form. 11. Dance tells quite a story.

10 Choose the best way to write sentence 1.

F Dancing is one of the oldest and liveliest of the arts.

G Dancing one of the oldest and liveliest of the arts.

H One of the oldest and liveliest of the arts are dancing.

J It is best as it is.

11 Choose the best way to write sentence 2.

A Pictures on cave walls there show primitive dance.

B Pictures on cave walls show that there were primitive dance.

C There are cave walls that show primitive dance pictures.

D It is best as it is.

12 **Choose the best way to write sentence 4.**

    F   Dance does for us.

    G   What does dance do for us?

    H   What does dance do for us!

    J   It is best as it is.

13 **Choose the best way to write sentence 6.**

    A   People bring it together in thought and feeling.

    B   It brings people together in thought and feeling.

    C   With thought and feeling, people bring it together.

    D   It is best as it is.

14 **Choose the best way to combine sentences 8 and 9.**

    F   Everyday life is told by her movement and religious history too.

    G   Her movements can tell about religious history and everyday life.

    H   Her movements can tell about religious history and they can tell about everyday life.

    J   It is best as it is.

15 **Choose the best way to write sentence 10.**

    A   Using any style or form.

    B   It can use any style or form.

    C   The dancer can use any style or form.

    D   It is best as it is.

16 **Where would this sentence best fit in the paragraph?**

It is an art that constantly changes, but the feelings dance expresses are timeless.

    F   after sentence 1

    G   after sentence 4

    H   after sentence 8

    J   after sentence 11

Directions: The article "Yo! Walk That Dog" is about an ancient game that is very popular today. Author Barbara Kerley gives readers a history of the yo-yo as well as some tips on how to play with it. Read the article, then read each question. Darken the circle for the correct answer.

YO! WALK THAT DOG

The yo-yo may seem like a modern toy, as American as apple pie, but it's actually very old. It may have been invented in the Philippines or in China, but as long ago as 450 B.C., it had reached Europe. A boy playing with what we now call a yo-yo is even shown on a bowl from ancient Greece.

It wasn't until the 1930s, however, that yo-yos became an American fad. Pedro Flores, a Filipino immigrant working in California, began to make and sell yo-yos in the 1920s. (The word *yo-yo* means "come back" in Filipino language.) A few years later, Flores sold his company to Donald Duncan, an American businessman. Duncan, an ingenious marketer, sent demonstrators called Duncan Champions around the country to show off yo-yo tricks and give out free instruction booklets. When kids saw the cool tricks, they wanted yo-yos for themselves.

Soon Duncan Champions were organizing contests across the country. Competing kids would perform tricks for points—ten if the trick was performed successfully on the first try, five for the second try. Whoever earned the most points won. In the case of a tie, first place went to the kid who could do the most Loop-the-Loops without stopping.

Yo-yos have remained popular for decades. In the 1950s Duncan's factory produced up to 60,000 every day. In Nashville in 1961, more yo-yos were sold than there were people living in the city.

With practice, anyone can learn yo-yo tricks and perform them well. The first thing you'll need to do is cut the yo-yo's string to the proper length. Place the yo-yo on the ground and pull the string up until it reaches just above your waist. Clip it, tie a slipknot, and slide it onto your middle finger, between the first and second knuckle. Wind up the string and hold your yo-yo in your palm. Flick it down, turning your hand over to catch it when it returns. Practice until you've mastered a smooth, comfortable rhythm. You're now ready to go to Sleep.

Sleeping is the basis for many tricks. Begin with the regular toss, but once the yo-yo leaves your hand, hold your wrist absolutely still. Instead of returning, the yo-yo should spin at the bottom of the string. A quick flip of the wrist will bring it back to you. If you have trouble sleeping, try a glass of warm milk at bedtime. If your yo-yo has trouble Sleeping, make sure your string isn't twisted up too tightly. Let the yo-yo unwind and gently untwist itself.

Practice Sleeping until you can do it for five seconds without waking up. Once you can do that, you're ready to Walk the Dog. Toss down a Sleeper, then gently place it on the floor. Like walking any dog on a leash, you'll need to follow along behind.

fad = something that is very popular for a short time

basis = starting point

17 What is a main idea of this passage?

A Yo-yo contests were first organized by Donald Duncan.

B In the 1950s, as many as 60,000 yo-yos were produced each day.

C Yo-yo tricks take a lot of practice.

D Today, children enjoy learning to do different tricks with the yo-yo, a toy dating back to ancient times.

18 Which picture shows the last trick described in the passage?

F

H

G

J

19 The author tells us that yo-yo games were probably first played in

   A ancient times

   B the 1920s

   C the 1950s

   D 1961

20 The author describes a popular yo-yo trick that is compared to

   F flying a kite

   G bowling

   H walking a dog

   J drinking a glass of milk

21 If two contestants were tied in a Duncan Champions yo-yo contest, how was the winner decided?

   A The winner was the contestant who could do the most tricks.

   B The winner was the contestant who did the most Loop-the-Loops without stopping.

   C The winner was the contestant who earned ten points.

   D The winner was the contestant who could Walk the Dog for ten minutes.

22 The passage says that <u>yo-yo</u> is a Filipino word that means

F go away

G come back

H loop-the-loop

J sleeping

23 Which information from the passage best supports the answer to question 22?

A the information that tells how to toss the yo-yo from the wrist

B the information that tells how to return the yo-yo to your hand

C the information about the game called Sleeping

D the information about rules for contestants

24 The author says that Duncan was an <u>ingenious</u> marketer.

The word <u>ingenious</u> probably means

F rich

G clever

H champion

J immigrant

25 Which piece of information in the passage best supports the answer to question 24 ?

A Flores sold his company to Donald Duncan.

B When kids saw the cool tricks, they wanted yo-yos for themselves.

C Soon, Duncan Champions were organizing contests around the country.

D A Filipino immigrant working in California began to make and sell yo-yos in 1920.

26 The author of the passage would probably agree that

F yo-yos are only for children

G yo-yos are only for adults

H Sleeping is a trick anyone can do

J Walk the Dog is most popular among Filipino children

27 If you wanted to learn more about the topic of the passage, which book would be most useful?

A *The Greek Olympics*

B *New Magic Tricks*

C *Factory Production in the 1950s*

D *The Klutz Yo-Yo Book*

Directions: Mr. Kane's class is working on reports about games. Read these questions. Darken the circle for the correct answer.

28 Choose the sentence that does <u>not</u> correctly combine both the sentences into one.

Mr. Kane's class visited the library.

The class learned about many games invented in the Philippines and China.

F Mr. Kane's class visited the library and learned about many games invented in the Philippines and China.

G Mr. Kane's class visited the library, where they learned about many games invented in the Philippines and China.

H On their visit to the library, Mr. Kane's class learned about games from the Philippines and China.

J Mr. Kane's class visited the library they learned about many games invented in the Philippines and China.

29 Which resource would be best for finding a map of the Philippines?

A

C

B

D

30 **A student in Mr. Kane's class plans to read an article about Chinese life. Under which heading of the article would he find information about games Chinese children play today?**

   F   Our Village

   G   A Day in the Life of a Chinese Lady

   H   Games and Recreation in China

   J   Ancient Games

31 **Choose the sentence that is written correctly.**

   A   The child wound the string and held the yo-yo in her palm.

   B   The yo-yo were her favorite toy.

   C   She use it almost every day.

   D   She keeped it in her toy chest with her other prized possessions.

32 **Choose the sentence that is written correctly.**

   F   Games that are too difficult to play.

   G   Until you get it right.

   H   Follow these simple instructions.

   J   Using a sharp flick of the wrist.

33 **Choose the sentence that needs to be corrected.**

   A   These ancient games still interest many people.

   B   New books about old and modern games are published every year.

   C   These books make fine gifts for both children and parents.

   D   Many children buy game books they learn the rules of different games.

Directions: Read this story about a little girl who does something daring. Then answer the questions that follow.

The Haircut

by Judith Herbst

Sophie stood behind the chain-link fence in her stupid pink dress. Her golden hair hung in tight banana curls. A pink satin ribbon held back some of them but certainly not all. Her black patent leather shoes had been polished, but now they were dull from the fine gray dust around home plate.

Stinky Mallory hit a grounder and tried to beat it out. His knickers were worn in the front from trying to beat out grounders. Sophie kept telling him to slide on his rear end, but Stinky ignored her. After all, this was baseball, and she was just a girl.

"Let me play!" she begged them every Saturday. "I'm good. I swing like Hack Wilson."

"Oh, big, fat deal!" Bernie Cohen had told her. "What did he do last year? Thirty homers? Ruth hit sixty!"

"Well, you can't get Babe Ruth to play on your dumb team," Sophie had said. "But you can get me."

"Yeah, maybe," said Stinky. "But we don't want you. Besides, you'd mess up your bee-you-ti-full dress."

"Go on home," said Tony DeLeo. "Bake a pie or something."

They burst out laughing, slapping each other on the back and spitting in the dirt, the way they had seen the Babe do it. Sophie made a face and backed away from the fence. "I can, too, hit," she murmured. "Better than all of you."

That night Sophie stared at her reflection in the mirror. She didn't want to be a boy, she decided. But it wasn't fair that she couldn't do boy things. How come life was like that? She wondered.

© Harcourt Achieve Inc. All rights reserved.

"Sophie!" her mother called out from the kitchen. Sophie could hear the water running in the sink. "Did you brush your hair?"

"Yes, mama!"

"One hundred strokes?"

"Yes, mama."

"Your hair is your crowning glory," her mother kept telling her, but Sophie wasn't so sure. Hair was just hair. Hair got in the way. It was a pain in the neck. You had to do stuff to it, brush it and curl it and tie it back. Sophie gathered her hair in one hand and held it away from her face. Her neck felt cool and free. Her face looked somehow...stronger. She let her hair fall back. It was so heavy, like a thick veil that women wore in faraway places like Persia.

Suddenly, a bubble of excitement rose in Sophie's chest. She knew what she was about to do. It scared her a little, but it felt just right. It was the summer of 1928, and she was twelve. It was time.

"WHAT HAVE YOU DONE?" screamed her mother the following morning. She looked as though she was about to faint.

Sophie shrugged. "Just a haircut," she said.

Sophie's mother staggered to a chair and sat down. Her mouth had dropped open like a trapdoor. "Sophie!" she squeaked. "Your beautiful hair! How could you?" She shook her head.

"It's only hair, mama, and besides, I like it much better this way."

"What are those clothes you're wearing?" said her mother, eyeing the brown tweed knickers Sophie had gotten from her brother's drawer.

"They're David's," said Sophie. "They fit pretty good, don't you think?"

Sophie's mother rolled her eyes. "I think you've gone crazy, she said. "I think you look like one of those dirty boys who play stickball in the street."

"You do?" said Sophie grinning. "Good, cause I do believe there's a game this afternoon."

34 The boys will not let Sophie play ball with them because

   F she's a girl

   G she's not a good hitter

   H her long hair won't fit in the baseball cap

   J she's not an official member of the team

35 What clue are we given in the story that Sophie will cut her hair?

   A Her mother tells her, "Your hair is your crowning glory."

   B She says her neck feels cool and free without it.

   C She wants to keep up with the fashions of 1928.

   D She is determined to be accepted by the boys on the team.

36 What is Sophie's strongest reason for cutting her hair?

   F She wants to look and feel more like a boy.

   G It is her way of rebelling against her mother.

   H She wants to surprise her brother.

   J She likes the way her face looks with short hair.

37 Why is Sophie's mother so surprised to see Sophie wearing knickers?

   A She hadn't remembered Sophie buying any.

   B She didn't think David's knickers would fit Sophie.

   C Girls almost always wore dresses in those days.

   D She had forbidden Sophie to borrow her brother's clothes.

38 Which word best describes Sophie?

   F determined

   G rude

   H disobedient

   J unhappy

39 What would be different in the story if it took place today instead of in 1928?

   A Boys would not tease girls.

   B Sophie could find a girls' baseball team to join.

   C Most girls of Sophie's age would have short hair.

   D Sophie could never surprise her mother by her actions.

STOP

Here is more about how people have fun.

Directions: Today girls have their own baseball teams. Several students from one girls' team made a poster to announce their first game of the season. There are some mistakes that need to be corrected. Read the poster and each question. Darken the circle for the correct answer.

SEASON OPENER BASEBALL GAME

Lakeside Elementary School
Wednesday, April 25th at 4:00 P.M.
Baseball Field

1. **Come see us play the Browning School who beats us last year.**

2. **See our improved team.**

3. **Watch us knock it out of the yard.**

4. **Don't miss the great game we'll play.**

---

40 Choose the best way to write sentence 1.

F See us play the Browning School who beated us last year.

G Who beats us last year? The Browning School!

H Come see us play the Browning School who beat us last year.

J Come see us play the Browning School who has beated us last year.

41 **Which sentence would best follow sentence 3?**

  A We lost four practice games.

  B We've been practicing all month.

  C The coach replaced two players.

  D We couldn't find new players this year.

42 **Choose the sentence that is written correctly.**

  F Our lineup will help you to not miss the great game we will play.

  G Watch us shut out Browning and cheer for our improved team.

  H Don't miss the great game we played against the Browning School who beat us last year.

  J The Browning School, beat us last year, saw our improved team.

43 **If you wanted to find out more about how to play baseball, which source would be the most helpful?**

  A    **C**

  B    **D**

44 The word <u>knock</u> probably means

    F play

    G hit

    H see

    J hear

45 Which idea will probably not come up when the coach talks to the team before the game?

    A how to avoid making mental errors

    B keeping your eye on the ball

    C what grades team members got

    D who will substitute for the pitcher

46 Which question would lead to a better understanding of how baseball is played?

    F Who invented the game?

    G Who are the most famous baseball players?

    H What are the official rules of the game?

    J What player set the world's record for home runs?

Directions: Here is a letter a girl wrote to the coach. There are some mistakes that need to be corrected. Read the letter. Then answer the questions.

Dear Coach Hardy,

I watched the team practice Wednesday. They were good. I wish I could play with them. Are there an opening on the team for me?

Sincerely yours,

Celine

47 **Choose the best way to write the first sentence of the letter.**

A I watch the team practicing Wednesday.

B On Wednesday, I watch the team practice.

C I am watching the team practicing Wednesday.

D It is best as it is.

48 **Choose the best way to write sentence 3.**

F I wish I to could play with them.

G I wish I could play with them two.

H I wish I could play with them to.

J It is best as it is.

49 **Choose the best way to write the last sentence.**

A Are there any opening on the team for me?

B On the team, are there an opening for me?

C Is there an opening on the team for me?

D It is best as it is.

Fables and Legends

Fables and legends are stories that have been told and retold for hundreds of years. The tales were first told aloud by storytellers to both adults and children. Some of the stories teach lessons about how to act, while others explain why things happen as they do. In this theme, you will read stories from different cultures. You will notice that these tales ask you to use your imagination and believe for a moment that strange things can "really" happen. So turn the page and jump into the timeless land of fables and legends.

Directions: Here is a Native American Indian legend. Read the story and answer the questions that follow.

THE MOON AND THE GREAT SNAKE

Once there was only one Snake in the whole world, and he was a big one. He was beautiful to look at, as he was painted with all the colors we know.

The Snake was in love with the Moon, and she knew it. This big Snake used to slither up a high hill and watch the Moon in the sky. She liked his looks, but she paid no attention to him. She was in love with her husband, the Sun.

One day, the Snake decided that the hill he was on wasn't high enough for the Moon to see him, so he found a higher one. Every night he climbed this high hill and waved his head to the Moon until, finally, she took a good look at him. After all, the Sun goes early to bed, and the Moon almost always leaves their lodge before the Sun comes home. One morning, quite early, the Moon loafed at her work a little in order to speak with the Snake. He quite enjoyed talking with her and she with him because the Snake said many enchanting things to her.

The next morning the Moon saw the Snake again, and this time she stopped to talk to him a long time—so long that the Sun had started out from their lodge before she reached home. He wondered what kept his wife so long. The Sun became suspicious and made up his mind to watch his wife

loafed = spent time doing little or nothing

to see what was making her late. Every morning the Sun left his lodge a little earlier than the day before, until one morning, just as he climbed a mountain, he saw the big Snake talking to the Moon. He became very angry, and you can't blame him. After all, his wife was wasting time with a Snake.

As soon as the Moon saw her husband, she ran away to their lodge. In no time the Sun had grabbed the Snake. My, the Sun was angry! He smashed the Snake into thousands of little pieces, each piece a different color from the different parts of the Snake's painted body. Each little piece turned into a little snake, just as you see them today. That is how so many snakes came into the world.

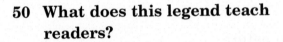

50 **What does this legend teach readers?**

F why the Moon cannot be seen in the daytime

G that the Sun can sink down to the earth

H why there are so many different kinds of snakes on Earth

J the exact position of the Sun and Moon in the sky

51 **What big mistake does the Snake make?**

A He thinks he is small enough to hide from the Sun.

B He falls in love with the Moon.

C He tries to make the Moon jealous.

D He tries to fly up to the Moon.

52 **In this passage, the word <u>enchanting</u> means**

F harmful

G confusing

H silly

J delightful

53 **What does <u>not</u> happen in this story?**

A The Sun becomes angry with the Snake.

B The Snake and the Moon get married.

C The Moon enjoys talking with the Snake.

D The Snake admires the Moon.

54 **Which best explains why the Moon becomes interested in the Snake?**

   F   The Moon is bored with her husband, the Sun.

   G   The Snake is very handsome.

   H   The Snake keeps on trying to get the Moon's attention.

   J   The Moon understands the Snake's true nature.

55 **Which best describes the main point of this story?**

   A   Love can overcome any challenge.

   B   Mind is more powerful than muscle.

   C   Remember who and what you are.

   D   All creatures are equal.

56 **The last paragraph shows that the American Indians believe**

   F   most snakes are poisonous

   G   the Moon is like a foolish woman

   H   the Sun is an enemy of all creatures

   J   there is a reason and place for everything in nature

57 **Choose the sentence that is written correctly.**

   A   The Snake thought the Moon were really in love with him.

   B   The Snake thought the Moon was really in love with him.

   C   The Snake thinks the Moon are really in love with him.

   D   The Snake thinked the Moon was really in love with him.

58 **Which sentences best support this topic sentence?**

People have always been afraid of snakes.

   F   Rabbits are much cuter, and kittens and puppies are cuddly. That is why most people prefer them as pets.

   G   The snake is often seen as evil. Perhaps we fear the way it slithers so quietly, or maybe we don't like its cold eyes and forked tongue.

   H   My cousin has a little green snake that is not scary at all. I like to hold him and let him wrap himself around my arm.

   J   Our neighborhood pet shop has a boa constrictor. The shop owner feeds the snake crickets and other insects.

Directions: "The Ostrich Feather" is a tale from Bushmen, people who live in the Kalahari Desert in southwest Africa. What you read may not seem real. But the Bushmen made up stories like this to help explain things they did not understand. Read the story, then answer the questions that follow.

The Ostrich Feather

by Elizabeth S. Helfman

A Bushman killed an ostrich and carried it home. Some of the ostrich's feathers were bloody and the Bushman's wife put them on nearby bushes to dry. Then the Bushman and his wife settled down to a meal of ostrich meat.

While they were eating, a little whirlwind came along and blew on the ostrich feathers. One little feather with blood on it was carried up into the sky, where it whirled around. Then it fell down out of the sky into the water, where it became wet. And suddenly it was no longer just an ostrich feather. It came alive as it lay in the water. It became ostrich flesh; feathers grew on it, and wings. Legs grew while it lay there and the new little ostrich walked out of the water and basked in the sun at the water's edge. All its feathers were black, because it was a little male ostrich.

When his feathers were dry the ostrich walked away from the water, unstiffening his legs and strengthening his feet. He lay down to rest while his breastbone became bone. Then he walked again and ate small young plants, because he was only a little ostrich. And he roared, hardening his ribs so they, too, would become bone.

The little ostrich let himself grow. His flesh became stronger and he felt heavy because his legs were big. He grew great strong feathers. Now he could roar strongly, for his ribs were big.

He was a grown-up ostrich with long wing feathers. He went home to where the big ostrich had been killed when he was one of its little feathers. There his wives laid eggs and he took good care of the eggs, because they were indeed his children.

So the dead ostrich came back to life because one little feather with a drop of blood on it whirled in the wind, dropped into the water, and came alive.

59 **The main idea of this passage is that**

A   a Bushman and his wife killed an ostrich

B   ostriches have short lives

C   an ostrich came back to life

D   ostriches have a special way of raising their young

60 **The story says, "While they were eating, a little <u>whirlwind</u> came along and blew on the ostrich feathers."**

Which of these words means the same as <u>whirlwind</u>?

F   snowflake

G   mild tornado

H   fan

J   Australian bird

61 **This tale was probably told because Bushmen**

A   were afraid of the ostrich

B   wanted more food

C   kept ostriches as pets

D   didn't know what makes life begin

62 **Which statement shows that the ostrich had feelings?**

F   He basked in the sun at the water's edge.

G   He roared to harden his ribs.

H   He went home to where the big ostrich had been killed.

J   He took good care of the eggs because they were his children.

63 **Which picture shows the ostrich feather whirling?**

A

B

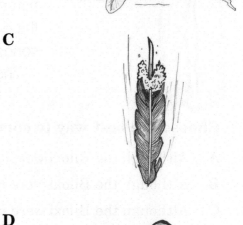

C

D

64 **Which of these best describes the theme of the story?**

F   beauty is all around us

G   seasons change

H   life goes on

J   nature is cruel

Directions: Here is a student's report on a well-known tale, "The Song That Comes From the Sea." It is a tale of heroism told about Native Americans. Some say it happened in what is now Mississippi. This version was told by the Biloxi Indians of Alabama. The report contains several mistakes that need correcting. Read the report and answer the questions that follow.

The Song That Comes From the Sea

1. The Biloxi were a great tribe. 2. They lived in peace and did their work without wars. 3. The tribes around them were not so peaceful. 4. The Choctaw were the most warlike of all. 5. One day the Choctaw Chief decided to go on the warpath against the Biloxi. 6. Although the Biloxi were not afraid. 7. They did not want war. 8. Rather than attacking the Choctaw, they decided to defend their homes and land. 9. They retreated and builded a fort on the edge of a great bay. 10. They played games and sang songs.

11. They tried to hold off the enemy as best they could.

65 Choose the best way to combine sentences 6 and 7.

A   Although the Biloxi were not afraid of war.

B   Although the Biloxi were not afraid and did not want war.

C   Although the Biloxi were not afraid, they did not want war.

D   It is best as it is.

66 Choose the best way to write sentence 9.

F   They retreat and build a fort on the edge of a great bay.

G   They retreated and build a fort on the edge of a great bay.

H   They retreated and built a fort on the edge of a great bay.

J   It is best as it is.

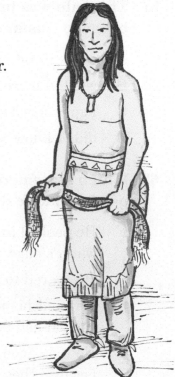

67 Which sentence does not belong in the paragraph?

A   sentence 2

B   sentence 5

C   sentence 8

D   sentence 10

Directions: Here is the second paragraph of the report.

1. The Biloxi fought a fierce battle. 2. Soon they ran out of food. 3. They had to battle another enemy, hunger. 4. They could not hunt, and their supplies were running low. 5. One day, the Biloxi chiefs met in a great council. 6. If they surrendered, it was certain death to everyone, men, women, and children.

68   Choose the best way to combine sentences 2 and 3.

F   They had to battle another enemy, hunger, as soon as they ran out of food.

G   They ran out of food as soon as they had to battle another enemy, hunger.

H   Running out of food, they had to battle another enemy, hunger.

J   Soon they ran out of food and had to battle another enemy, hunger.

69   Choose where this sentence best fits in the paragraph.

They had to discuss the facts about their situation.

A   after sentence 3

B   after sentence 4

C   after sentence 5

D   after sentence 6

Directions: Here is the last paragraph of the report.

1. They all saw only one way out, the sea!
2. They would all walk together into the sea.
3. There the Choctaw could not attack them.
4. There they would have no fear of hunger or violence there they would find peace. 5. The brave Biloxi showed how men and women could go from this world to another without fear.

70   Choose the sentence that contains two complete thoughts and should be written as two sentences.

   F   sentence 2
   G   sentence 3
   H   sentence 4
   J   sentence 5

71   If the student who wrote the report wanted to find more information about the Biloxi tribe in the library, it would be best to look under

   A   the tribal name
   B   Mississippi
   C   war
   D   Native American reservations

Directions: This is a story of a young wife, her husband, and her husband's parents. Read the story. Then answer the questions that follow.

The Priest's Towel

by David Conger

"When I was living in Japan many years ago," said Mr. Miller, "one day I was talking with the wife of a friend of mine, and she told me that she didn't like her husband's mother." In Japan the eldest son supports his parents when they are old. Very often the parents, the son, and his wife all live in the same house together. Many times the husband's wife and his mother don't get along. It doesn't necessarily mean that either of them are bad—they just don't get along.

"Well, the wife of my friend didn't get along with her husband's mother. She said it reminded her of a story, and she told it to me. It goes like this…"

Long ago there was a young wife who lived with her husband and her husband's parents. This wife and her mother-in-law didn't get along. Day and night they fought and argued.

One day, the young wife made some *mochi*. *Mochi* are small cakes made from pounded rice. The kind young woman gave some of the *mochi* to a priest who lived at the nearby temple. In Japan, the priests depend on the generosity of other people, and they often go door to door asking for food and clothes. The Japanese believe that whoever donates something to a priest will be blessed. Anyway, the young woman gave the priest some of the *mochi* she had just made.

When the mother-in-law found out about this, she gave the wife a good tongue-lashing. "Do you think that my son is made of money?" she yelled. "We can't afford to give food to every good-for-nothing priest that comes along. You go after that young man and get the *mochi* back."

The wife went down the road after the priest and, although she was very embarrassed, asked the priest for the *mochi*. The priest was very good about the whole thing and returned them. Because the young wife had been kind to him, he also gave her a small towel to wash her face with.

The young wife used the towel to wash her face every day. Little by little she became more and more beautiful. But when her mother-in-law saw how beautiful she was getting, she took the towel away from her.

After that, the mother began to use the towel every day, but instead of becoming more beautiful, she gradually began to have the face of a horse. Even though her mother-in-law had been very cruel to her, the young wife felt sorry for her. She went to the temple to ask the priest for his help. The priest told her that if her mother-in-law would use the other side of the cloth, her face would return to normal.

The young wife went back to her mother-in-law and told her what the priest had said. The mother followed the priest's instructions, and her face changed back to its original form.

The mother-in-law began to realize how mean she had been to her daughter-in-law, and how kind her daughter-in-law had been to her.
After that the mother was always kind to her son's wife, and they got along very well.

72 The main idea of this story is

F the poverty of Japanese priests

G Mr. Miller's knowledge of Japanese customs

H a mother-in-law's rudeness

J getting along with others

73 What important lesson did the mother-in-law learn?

A don't borrow another person's property

B it is better to be kind

C it pays to be mean

D don't give away food

74 According to the author, why does the oldest son in a Japanese family take care of his parents?

    F   the government pays him to do so

    G   he knows it is his duty

    H   there is a law that says he must

    J   his wife demands it

75 As the word <u>donates</u> is used in this story, it probably means

    A   cooks

    B   asks for food and clothes

    C   prays

    D   gives freely

76 When the young girl used the towel every day, she became more beautiful. When the mother used the towel, she became ugly because she

    F   loved her son too much

    G   was cruel to her daughter-in-law

    H   was not loved by her husband

    J   needed a softer towel

77 Which is the best reason why the mother-in-law and wife did not get along?

    A   The daughter was jealous.

    B   The mother-in-law was jealous.

    C   There was no food in the house.

    D   The son was never home.

78 Choose the sentence that best combines both the sentences into one.

Use this towel every day.

You will find joy and beauty in your life.

    F   You will find joy and beauty in your life if you use this towel every day.

    G   Use this towel every day, but you will find joy and beauty in your life.

    H   You will find joy and beauty in your life although you use this towel every day.

    J   To use this towel every day, you will find joy and beauty in your life.

Directions: In this theme, you have read fables and legends that were told to explain mysterious events or teach important lessons. Here are two paragraphs that tell how a dog tricked himself out of a juicy bone. After you read them, answer the questions.

One day a hungry dog was delighted to find a juicy bone. He took the bone to the river to wash it off. When he looked into the water, he saw something surprising. _____. Why, that bone looked even bigger than the one in his own mouth!

79 Choose the sentence that best completes the story.

   A   A silvery fish was leaping above the ripples.

   B   An ugly bullfrog with a gaping mouth stared up at him.

   C   Another dog also had a bone in its mouth.

   D   A giant trout had a smaller fish in its jaws.

Directions: Here is the second paragraph.

The greedy dog quickly made a plan. He would make a grab for the other dog's bone, and then he would have two bones. He opened his mouth wide to get that delicious-looking treat. _____. Surprised, the dog sat down on the riverbank and howled. He had no meal, but he was a wiser dog.

80 Choose the sentence that best completes the story.

   F   He grabbed the bone and ate it right up.

   G   His bone fell into the water and sank to the bottom.

   H   The dog in the water gave him the bone and ran away.

   J   The other dog bit him and the two fought for an hour.

Section
B

Mathematics

About Section B: Mathematics

This section of the book has been developed to refresh basic skills, familiarize your child with test formats and directions, and teach test-taking strategies. This section of the book is divided into three components: Lessons, Review Tests, and Comprehensive Test.

Note: In order to answer some of the problems in this section, students will need a ruler with measurements marked off in both inches and centimeters. A ruler is provided on page 101.

Lessons

There is one lesson for each of the nine math skills assessed on the CTB-TerraNova Mathematics tests. Each lesson contains:

- *Try This*: a skill strategy that enables your child to approach each lesson in a logical manner

- *Sample*: to familiarize your child with test-taking items

- *Think It Through* : the correct answer to the sample item and an explanation that tells why the correct answer is correct and why the incorrect answers are wrong

- two practice questions based on the lesson and modeled on the kinds of items found on the CTB-TerraNova

Review Test

The lessons are followed by a short Review Test that covers all the skills in the lessons. This section is designed to provide your child with independent practice that will familiarize him or her with the testing situation.

Comprehensive Test

The last component in this section is a Comprehensive Test. This test gives your child an opportunity to take a test under conditions that parallel those he or she will face when taking the CTB-TerraNova Mathematics test.

In order to simulate the CTB-TerraNova test as closely as possible, we have suggested time limits for the Comprehensive Test. This will enable your child to experience test taking under the same structured conditions that apply when achievement tests are administered. Furthermore, your child will have a final opportunity to apply the skills he or she has learned in this section prior to taking the CTB-TerraNova.

The recommended time limits are:
  Part 1: 15 minutes
  Part 2: 45 minutes

Have your child use the Mathematics Test Answer Sheet on page 111 to record the answers for this comprehensive test.

Answer Key

The Answer Key at the back of the book contains the answers for all the problems found in this section.

Mathematics

Directions: Read each question carefully. Darken the circle for the correct answer.

 Read word problems carefully. Look for clue words that help you figure out the operations you should use.

Sample

Barton brought $8.48 in pennies to a bank. He asked the teller for dimes in return. How many dimes did he get?

A   80

B   84

C   85

D   848

 The correct answer is <u>B</u>, <u>84</u>. Since each dime is worth $0.10, 84 × $0.10 = $8.40. After receiving his dimes, Barton will have 8 pennies left over.

---

1   Which shape is exactly one-third shaded?

   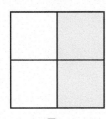   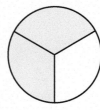   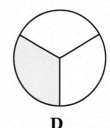

      A   B   C   D

2   The table below shows the attendance at Rockets baseball games five days this week. On which day was attendance second greatest?

F   Tuesday

G   Wednesday

H   Thursday

J   Friday

Day	Attendance
Monday	8,151
Tuesday	8,760
Wednesday	9,053
Thursday	9,111
Friday	9,035

Answers

S Ⓐ Ⓑ Ⓒ Ⓓ   2 Ⓕ Ⓖ Ⓗ Ⓙ

1 Ⓐ Ⓑ Ⓒ Ⓓ

STOP

Directions: Read each question carefully. Darken the circle for the correct answer.

Rounding money amounts to the nearest dollar allows you to estimate sums and differences quickly.

Sample

Felicita had soup and a sandwich for lunch. The sandwich cost $4.95 and the total bill was $8.90. Which is the best estimate for the price of the soup?

A $3

B $4

C $5

D $12

E $14

The correct answer is <u>B</u>, <u>$4</u>. Subtract the cost of the sandwich from the total cost to find the cost of the soup: $8.90 − $4.95 ≈ $9 − $5 = $4.

---

1 **840 ÷ 250 =**

A 3.36

B 33.6

C 336

D 590

E None of these

2 There are three grades at Fairview School. The table below shows the number of students in each grade. One day last January, 68 students were absent. How many students were in school that day?

F 44

G 152

H 288

J 298

Grade	Number of Students
4th	112
5th	124
6th	120

STOP

Answers
S Ⓐ Ⓑ Ⓒ Ⓓ Ⓔ   2 Ⓕ Ⓖ Ⓗ Ⓙ
1 Ⓐ Ⓑ Ⓒ Ⓓ Ⓔ

Lesson 3: Operation Concepts

Directions: Read each question carefully. Darken the circle for the correct answer.

Try This

When a word problem contains a great deal of information, try working through it step-by-step.

Sample

A carton contains 24 boxes. Each box contains 120 packs. Each pack contains 4 buttons. How many buttons are in a carton?

A   148

B   480

C   1,152

D   2,880

E   None of these

Think It Through

The correct answer is <u>E</u>, <u>None of these</u>. Since each pack contains 4 buttons, each box contains 120 × 4 = 480 buttons. Then, since each carton contains 24 boxes, each carton contains 24 × 480 = 11,520 buttons.

---

1   Look at the problem below. Which symbol goes in the box to give the *smallest* answer?

96 ☐ 1 =

A   +

B   ÷

C   ×

D   −

2   Which number sentence could be used to find the cost of 8 box seats?

F $18 × 8 = _____

G $18 ÷ 8 = _____

H $18 + 8 = _____

J $18 − 8 = _____

Box seats	$18
Reserved seats	$12
General Admission	$9
Bleachers	$6

Answers

S   Ⓐ Ⓑ Ⓒ Ⓓ Ⓔ   2   Ⓕ Ⓖ Ⓗ Ⓙ

1   Ⓐ Ⓑ Ⓒ Ⓓ

STOP

Lesson 4: Measurement

Directions: Read each question carefully. Darken the circle for the correct answer.

When a problem has a picture, label the picture to help you solve the problem.

Sample

Maribel plants corn in a field measuring 80 feet by 90 feet. What is the perimeter of her corn field?

90 feet

80 feet

A 170 feet

B 240 feet

C 340 feet

D 7,200 feet

Think It Through The correct answer is C, 340 feet. Counting lengths around the four sides, perimeter = 80 + 90 + 80 + 90 = 340 feet.

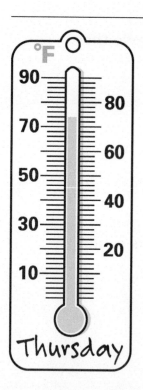

Thursday

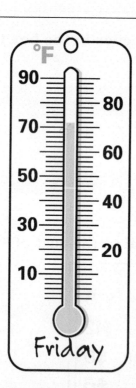

Friday

1 Look at the two thermometers. How did the temperature change?

A On Friday, it was 2 degrees colder than on Thursday.

B On Friday, it was 1 degree colder than on Thursday.

C On Friday, it was 2 degrees warmer than on Thursday.

D On Friday, it was 1 degree warmer than on Thursday.

2 Which holds the least?

F a one-cup bowl

G a one-ounce bowl

H a one-pint bowl

J a one-quart bowl

Answers
S Ⓐ Ⓑ Ⓒ Ⓓ   2 Ⓕ Ⓖ Ⓗ Ⓙ

70 1 Ⓐ Ⓑ Ⓒ Ⓓ

STOP

Lesson 5: Geometry and Spatial Sense

Directions: Read each question carefully. Darken the circle for the correct answer.

Try This When you are asked how a figure changes, you can draw it on scrap paper. Then fold it, turn it, or slide it.

Sample

The letter shown is flipped across the line below it. The figure that results is flipped across the line to its right. What figure results then?

Think It Through The correct answer is C, W. When a figure is flipped across a line below it, top becomes bottom and bottom becomes top. When a figure is flipped across a line next to it, left becomes right and right becomes left. In this example, the second flip does not change the figure since left and right are the same in that figure.

A   B   C   D

---

1   Which figure does not have a line of symmetry?

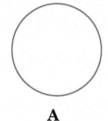

A   B   C   D

2   What is the area of the shaded triangle?

   F   3 square units

   G   4 square units

   H $4\frac{1}{2}$ square units

   J   6 square units

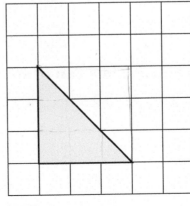

☐ = 1 square unit

Answers

S   Ⓐ Ⓑ ● Ⓓ   2   Ⓕ Ⓖ Ⓗ Ⓙ

1   Ⓐ Ⓑ Ⓒ Ⓓ

········· Lesson 6: Data Analysis, Statistics, and Probability

Directions: Read each question carefully. Darken the circle for the correct answer.

Try This

Before you try to solve a word problem, make sure you understand all the words in it.

Sample

Martina's grades on her last four social studies exams were 80, 90, 90, and 96. What was her average grade?

A 89

B 90

C 91

D 96

The correct answer is <u>A</u>, <u>89</u>. To find the average grade, add the four grades together and divide by 4: $\dfrac{80 + 90 + 96 + 90}{4} = \dfrac{356}{4} = 89$

The graph shows the price of a can of soda at four different stores. Study the graph and use it to answer problems 1 and 2.

1 At which store is a can of soda least expensive?

   A Morton's

   B Sam's

   C K&H

   D Filomena's

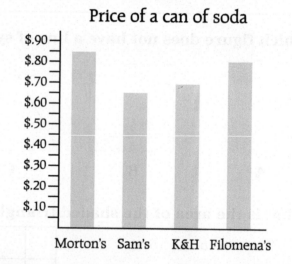

Price of a can of soda

2 How much more expensive is a can of soda at Morton's than at K&H?

   F 5 cents

   G 10 cents

   H 15 cents

   J 20 cents

© Harcourt Achieve Inc. All rights reserved.

Answers

S Ⓐ Ⓑ Ⓒ Ⓓ   2 Ⓕ Ⓖ Ⓗ Ⓙ

72 1 Ⓐ Ⓑ Ⓒ Ⓓ

STOP

Lesson 7: Patterns, Functions, and Algebra

Directions: Read each question carefully. Darken the circle for the correct answer.

Try This

When problems are about patterns, look for a rule that can help you explain how to go from one step to the next.

Sample

Look at the pattern below. What number comes next?

1, 2, 4, 7, 11, _____

A   12

B   15

C   16

D   18

Think It Through

The correct answer is <u>C</u>, 16. The rule is that the amount you add to get the next number increases by 1 as you move along. So, 1 + 1 = 2, 2 + 2 = 4, 4 + 3 = 7, 7 + 4 = 11, and 11 + 5 = 16.

---

1   The table below shows four examples of a new operation, #. This operation is not just addition, subtraction, multiplication, or division. It somehow combines two or more of those operations.

Study the table to explain how # works. What is 5 # 5?

A   24

B   25

C   26

D   28

$$2 \# 3 = 7$$
$$4 \# 1 = 5$$
$$6 \# 8 = 49$$
$$4 \# 2 = 9$$

2   If 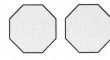 represents one whole unit, which figure represents one-half unit?

F   G   H   J

Answers

S Ⓐ Ⓑ Ⓒ Ⓓ   2 Ⓕ Ⓖ Ⓗ Ⓙ

1 Ⓐ Ⓑ Ⓒ Ⓓ

73

Lesson 8: Problem Solving and Reasoning

Directions: Read each question carefully. Darken the circle for the correct answer.

Try This Read word problems carefully to make sure you are answering the question being asked. Sometimes a word overlooked makes you answer a different question.

Sample

The figure below represents the ceiling Martha is painting. The shaded portion was painted today using one quart of paint. How many more quarts will Martha use to finish painting the ceiling?

A   4 quarts

B   3 quarts

C   2 quarts

D   1 quart

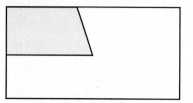

 **Think It Through** The correct answer is <u>B</u>, <u>3 quarts</u>. Since the portion already painted is about one-quarter of the ceiling, about 4 quarts are needed for the entire job. That means 3 more quarts will be used.

---

1   $\square \times 12 =$

Any whole number can be placed in the box. What can you determine about the answer?

A   The answer must be even.

B   The answer must be less than 100.

C   The answer must be greater than 12.

D   The answer may be 50.

2   Maureen has six brothers and sisters. Each of her sisters has 3 sisters. How many brothers does Maureen have?

F   2

G   3

H   4

J   6

Answers

S   Ⓐ Ⓑ Ⓒ Ⓓ   2   Ⓕ Ⓖ Ⓗ Ⓙ

74   1   Ⓐ Ⓑ Ⓒ Ⓓ

...... Lesson 9: Communication

Directions: Read each question carefully. Darken the circle for the correct answer.

Try This

When a problem asks you to check figures for a certain property, make sure you understand exactly what the property is before looking at the answer choices.

Sample

Which street sign shows an equilateral polygon?

Think It Through

The correct answer is <u>A</u>, <u>Stop Sign</u>. In an equilateral figure, all sides have the same length. This is not true in the two other signs.

None of these

A   B   C   D

---

1   Mrs. Brown's classroom number is an odd number less than 120. Which number could it be?

    A   116

    B   118

    C   123

    D   125

    E   None of these

2   Buster kept track of the number of movies he saw each summer using a tally chart. Between which two years did Buster's movie watching increase the most?

    F   1997 and 1998

    G   1996 and 1997

    H   1995 and 1996

    J   1994 and 1995

Summer	Movies watched
1994	/ / /
1995	++++ / / /
1996	++++ ++++ /
1997	++++ ++++ / /
1998	++++ ++++ ++++ /

Answers

Directions: Read each question. Darken the circle for the correct answer.

Sample

$16 \times 0.15 =$

A 0.24

B 2.4

C 24

D 240

E None of these

---

1 4,607
  + 298

A 4,995

B 4,905

C 4,895

D 4,805

E None of these

2 $\frac{4}{5} - \frac{3}{5} =$

F $\frac{7}{5}$

G $\frac{2}{0}$

H $\frac{1}{10}$

J $\frac{2}{5}$

K None of these

3 Five friends bought tickets for a school play. The total cost was $20. How much did each friend pay?

A $4

B $5

C $15

D $20

E None of these

Answers

S ⓐ ⓑ ⓒ ⓓ ⓔ   2 ⓕ ⓖ ⓗ ⓙ ⓚ

76 1 ⓐ ⓑ ⓒ ⓓ ⓔ   3 ⓐ ⓑ ⓒ ⓓ ⓔ

4 A can of tennis balls holds 3 balls. A carton holds 48 cans. How many tennis balls are there in a carton?

    F 51

    G 124

    H 134

    J 144

5 Which of the numbers in the set is not equivalent to the others?
$\{\frac{1}{4}, 2.5\%, 0.25, \frac{25}{100}\}$

    A $\frac{1}{4}$

    B 2.5%

    C 0.25

    D $\frac{25}{100}$

6 Which most likely states an incorrect length?

    F A house is 20 feet high.

    G A man is 6 feet tall.

    H A tomato is 8 inches wide.

    J A magazine is $\frac{1}{2}$ inch thick.

For problems 7 and 8 use estimation to find the best answer.

7 0.48×806

    A 0

    B 200

    C 400

    D 800

8 On her last fill-up, Maria recorded the information shown here. What was Maria's miles per gallon?

    F 3 miles per gallon

    G 30 miles per gallon

    H 300 miles per gallon

    J 3,000 miles per gallon

Miles driven   312
Gallons of gas   10.2

Answers

4 Ⓕ Ⓖ Ⓗ Ⓙ   6 Ⓕ Ⓖ Ⓗ Ⓙ   8 Ⓕ Ⓖ Ⓗ Ⓙ

5 Ⓐ Ⓑ Ⓒ Ⓓ   7 Ⓐ Ⓑ Ⓒ Ⓓ

9 Where would $\frac{1}{6}$ go on the number line?

A   Point A

B   Point B

C   Point C

D   Point D

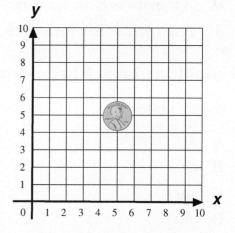

10 Which figure has a line of symmetry?

F G H J

F   G   H   J

11 It is now 7:45 A.M. School begins in exactly 50 minutes. When does school begin?

A   8:45 A.M.

B   8:35 A.M.

C   8:25 A.M.

D   8:15 A.M.

12 A penny is placed at the point (5, 5) on a coordinate grid. The penny is moved west 3 units and then north 4 units. At what point is the penny now?

F   (2, 9)

G   (2, 1)

H   (8, 9)

J   (8, 1)

13 Crystal paid for $43.24 worth of groceries with a $50 bill. Which number sentence could be used to find the change Crystal received?

A $50 \times 43.24 =$ _____

B $50 \div 43.24 =$ _____

C $50 + 43.24 =$ _____

D $50 - 43.24 =$ _____

Answers

9 Ⓐ Ⓑ Ⓒ Ⓓ   11 Ⓐ Ⓑ Ⓒ Ⓓ   13 Ⓐ Ⓑ Ⓒ Ⓓ

10 Ⓕ Ⓖ Ⓗ Ⓙ   12 Ⓕ Ⓖ Ⓗ Ⓙ

14 Which number comes next in the pattern?

3, 4, 6, 7, 9, 10, ?

F   11

G   12

H   13

J   14

15 The box below gives three clues about a number. What is the number?

> The number is odd.
>
> The number is greater than 40 and less than 50.
>
> The number is divisible by 7.

A   42

B   45

C   47

D   49

16 Which list shows the three rectangles in order from greatest area to least area?

F   rectangle C, rectangle A, rectangle B

G   rectangle C, rectangle B, rectangle A

H   rectangle B, rectangle C, rectangle A

J   rectangle A, rectangle B, rectangle C

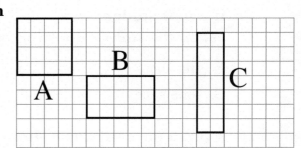

17 Which is *not* equivalent to 4 pints?

A   32 ounces

B   8 cups

C   2 quarts

D $\frac{1}{2}$ gallon

18 Which number can be placed in the box to make the inequality true?

$\square$ < 49.8?

F   49.008

G   49.8

H   49.9

J   50.1

Answers

14 Ⓕ Ⓖ Ⓗ Ⓙ   16 Ⓕ Ⓖ Ⓗ Ⓙ   18 Ⓕ Ⓖ Ⓗ Ⓙ

15 Ⓐ Ⓑ Ⓒ Ⓓ   17 Ⓐ Ⓑ Ⓒ Ⓓ

P᷍izza Party

Students were planning a pizza party. Everyone was asked how many slices they would eat. Study the graph and use it to answer problems 19 through 21.

19 How many more students said they wanted one slice than said they wanted three slices?

A 2

B 4

C 8

D 24

How Many Slices of Pizza Do You Want?

20 If a new student was asked the survey question, what response would be most likely?

F no slices   **H** two slices

G one slice   **J** three slices

21 A pizza pie contains 8 slices. Using the information in the graph, how many pies should be ordered?

A 10 pies   **C** 12 pies

B 11 pies   **D** 13 pies

Answers

19 Ⓐ Ⓑ Ⓒ Ⓓ   **21** Ⓐ Ⓑ Ⓒ Ⓓ

20 Ⓕ Ⓖ Ⓗ Ⓙ

COMPREHENSIVE TEST | Mathematics

Directions: Read each sample. Darken the circle for the correct answer. Remember to use the answer sheet on page 111 to fill in your answers.

Sample A

$$\begin{array}{r} 56 \\ +\ 34 \\ \hline \end{array}$$

A 80

B 90

C 22

D 32

E None of these

Sample B

Mr. Todd purchased movie tickets for himself and his three children. How much did he spend in all?

Ticket Prices	
Adult	$8.00
Child	$5.50

F $24.50

G $22.00

H $32.00

J $29.50

Go

Sample C

Use the inch side of your ruler to solve this problem. Remember to use the answer sheet on page 111 to fill in your answers.

How many inches wide is the photograph?

   A   3 inches

   B   4 inches

   C   5 inches

   D   6 inches

1 $118 \times 200 =$

    A 22,600

    B 23,600

    C 226,000

    D 236,000

    E None of these

2 $\begin{array}{r} 1.309 \\ + 2.792 \\ \hline \end{array}$

    F 3.001

    G 3.101

    H 4.001

    J 4.101

    K None of these

3 $\frac{2}{15} + \frac{11}{15} =$

    A $\frac{12}{15}$

    B $\frac{13}{30}$

    C $\frac{22}{225}$

    D $\frac{13}{15}$

    E None of these

4 $432 \div 21 =$

    F 20

    G 20 R 2

    H 21

    J 21 R 12

    K None of these

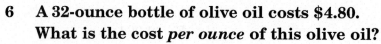

A Trip to the Supermarket

Amy went shopping for groceries for her family's holiday dinner. Do problems 5 through 8.

5 Amy purchased 6 pounds of potatoes that cost $0.59 per pound. How much did the potatoes cost in all?

    A $6.59   **C** $3.54

    B $6.50   **D** $3.04

6 A 32-ounce bottle of olive oil costs $4.80. What is the cost *per ounce* of this olive oil?

    F $0.15   **H** $4.47

    G $1.50   **J** $5.11

7 Amy arrived at the store at 2:45 P.M. She spent 50 minutes shopping. What time was it when she left?

    A 3:40 P.M.

    B 3:35 P.M.

    C 3:30 P.M.

    D 3:25 P.M.

8 The total bill for groceries was $67.83. Amy paid with a $100 bill. How much change did she receive?

    F $33.27

    G $33.17

    H $32.27

    J $32.17

For problems 9 through 13, use estimation to choose the best answer.

9 0.48×206

The answer is closest to

A   0

B   50

C   100

D   200

10 $8.67 + 1.35$

The answer is closest to

F   12

G   11

H   10

J   9

11 Mr. Underwood purchased three cans of coffee that each cost $5.99. About how much change should he expect from a $20 bill?

A $2

B $1

C $3

D $14

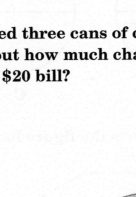

12 $14,579 \div 138$

The answer is closest to

F   10

G   100

H   1,000

J   10,000

13 The bill at a restaurant was $39.28. Martina left a $6 tip for the waitress. About what percent tip did Martina leave?

A   1.5%

B   6%

C   10%

D   15%

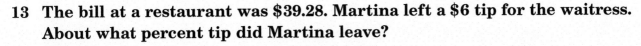

STOP

14 **Which statement is most likely incorrect?**

   F   A tomato weighs 6 ounces.

   G   A cat weighs 6 pounds.

   H   A boy weighs 60 pounds.

   J   A stereo weighs 600 pounds.

15 **Students were asked in a survey which fruit they liked best: apple, banana, or orange. Apple was the favorite and banana the least favorite. Which graph shows this result?**

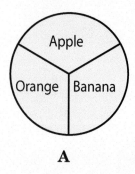 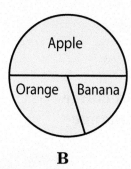 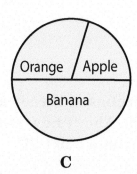 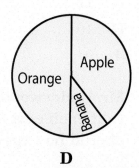

     A   **B**   **C**   **D**

16 **How many lines of symmetry does the figure have?**

   F   0

   G   1

   H   2

   J   3

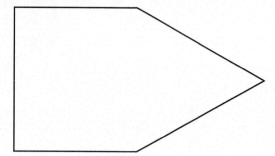

17 In the set of numbers shown, three of the numbers are equivalent.

$\{\frac{3}{2}, 1.05, 150\% \ 1\frac{1}{2}\}$

Which number is *not* equivalent to the rest?

A $\frac{3}{2}$

B 1.05

C 150%

D $1\frac{1}{2}$

18 Which point best shows where 175 would be placed on the number line?

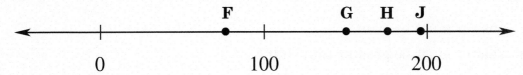

F point F

G point G

H point H

J point J

19 Which shape has exactly one-third shaded?

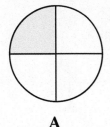 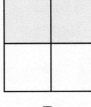  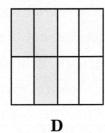

   A   B   C   D

20 Which number comes next in the pattern?

1, 3, 9, 27, ___

F 45

G 54

H 61

J 81

21 A whole number greater than 10 is placed in the box. What can you conclude about the answer to the problem?

$6 \times \square =$

A The answer must be even.

B The answer must be greater than 100.

C The answer must be less than 1,000.

D The answer must end in a zero.

22 A hot dog is $\frac{1}{2}$ foot long, an ear of corn is 8 inches long, and a stick of licorice is $\frac{1}{4}$ yard long. How are these items ordered from longest to shortest?

F licorice, corn, hot dog

G corn, licorice, hot dog

H hot dog, corn, licorice

J hot dog, licorice, corn

23 Which number sentence could *not* be used to find the cost of 3 tickets?

A $6 \times 3 =$ ___

B $6 + 6 + 6 =$ ___

C $3 \times 6 =$ ___

D $6 + 3 =$ ___

Tickets

~

$6.00
per person

24 Look at the problem below. Which symbol goes in the box to give the *greatest* answer?

44 ☐ 4 =

F +

G ÷

H ×

J –

25 Which shape has exactly six sides?

A quadrilateral

B pentagon

C hexagon

D octagon

26 What is another name for a 90° angle?

F acute angle

G right angle

H obtuse angle

J straight angle

27 The table shows how to convert a Celsius temperature to its equivalent Fahrenheit temperature.

1. Multiply the temperature by 1.8
2. Add 32 to the result

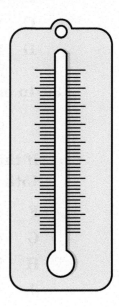

What is the equivalent Fahrenheit temperature for 20° Celsius?

A 58°

B 68°

C 93.6°

D 35.6°

Pet Fair

The students at the James K. Polk School held a pet fair. Some students brought their pets in for visitors to meet and other students prepared exhibits. Answer problems 28 through 33 about the pet fair.

28 The Pet Fair begins at 6:30 P.M. and ends at 9:15 P.M. on Friday night. How long is it that night?

    F   2 hours 15 minutes

    G   2 hours 45 minutes

    H   3 hours 15 minutes

    J   3 hours 45 minutes

29 As of 8 P.M., 120 people had visited the Pet Fair. The students' goal was 200 visitors. Which number sentence could be used to find how many more must visit to meet the goal?

    A $200 - 120 =$

    B $200 + 120 =$

    C $120 - 200 =$

    D $120 \div 200 =$

30 In order, the first 8 pets that Mr. Thurber visited were

    cat, dog, bird, snake, cat, dog, bird, snake

If this pattern continues, what will the 15th pet be that Mr. Thurber visits?

    F   cat

    G   dog

    H   bird

    J   snake

Visitors were asked what they liked best about the Pet Fair. The graph below shows their answers. Study it and then use it to answer problems 31 through 33.

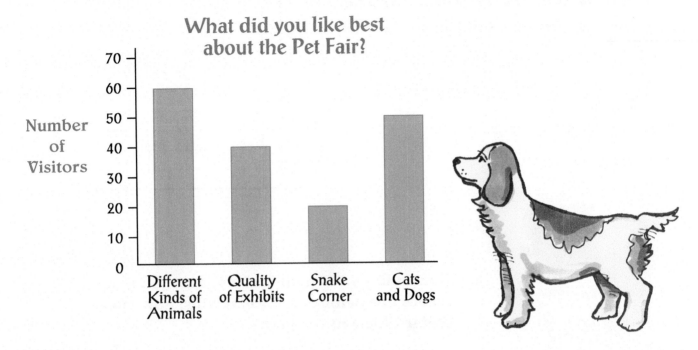

What did you like best about the Pet Fair?

Number of Visitors

Different Kinds of Animals — 60
Quality of Exhibits — 40
Snake Corner — 20
Cats and Dogs — 51

31 **Which answer was given by the most visitors?**

A Different Kinds of Animals

B Quality of Exhibits

C Snake Corner

D Cats and Dogs

32 **How many more visitors liked Cats and Dogs better than Snake Corner?**

F 40

G 30

H 20

J 10

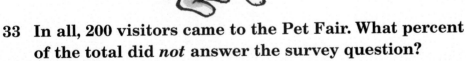

33 **In all, 200 visitors came to the Pet Fair. What percent of the total did *not* answer the survey question?**

A 85%

B 30%

C 17%

D 15%

34 Starting with a penny at the point (5, 3), move it up 3 units. Then move the penny to the left 2 units. At what point is the penny now?

F   (3, 6)

G   (3, 0)

H   (8, 5)

J   (8, 1)

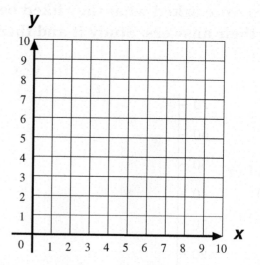

35 Dawan has 4,567 pennies in a large jar. If she trades her pennies for dollar bills, how many dollar bills will she get?

A   4

B   5

C   45

D   46

36 Valentine's Day chocolates are packaged in a box with 2 layers. Each layer contains 24 chocolates. The boxes are sold to stores in cartons containing 36 boxes. How many chocolates are in a carton?

F   62

G   864

H   866

J   1,728

37 The attendance at a baseball game was posted on the scoreboard.

What is this amount rounded to the nearest 100?

A 32,000

B 32,300

C 32,400

D 32,370

38 What is the area of the shaded figure?

F 17 square units

G 19 square units

H 21 square units

J 24 square units

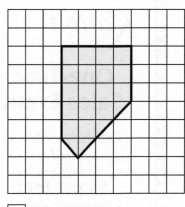

$\square$ = 1 square unit

39 Read the statements in the table to answer the question.

> Nicki has five brothers.
> Katy has two more brothers than Pilar.
> Pilar has three fewer brothers than Nicki.

How many brothers does Katy have?

A 5

B 4

C 3

D 2

40 One year, December 6 was the first Tuesday of the month. What was the last Tuesday in December that year?

F   December 26

G   December 27

H   December 28

J   December 31

41 Which statement is true about an isosceles triangle?

A   Two sides are equal in length.

B   All sides have the same length.

C   All sides have different lengths.

D   All angles are the same size.

42 A video store was running a special.

Ed has an old home movie that is 2,500 feet long. How much will it cost Ed to have it converted to video?

F $12.50

G $25.00

H $125.00

J $250.00

43 **Blaise drew a number chart from 1 to 100 as shown below.**

1	2	3	4	5	6	7	8	9	10
11	12	13	14	15	16	17	18	19	20
21	22	23	24	25	26	27	28	29	30
31	32	33	34	35	36	37	38	39	40
41	42	43	44	45	46	47	48	49	50
51	52	53	54	55	56	57	58	59	60
61	62	63	64	65	66	67	68	69	70
71	72	73	74	75	76	77	78	79	80
81	82	83	84	85	86	87	88	89	90
91	92	93	94	95	96	97	98	99	100

He then decided to shade in all the multiples of 4.
What pattern will Blaise get?

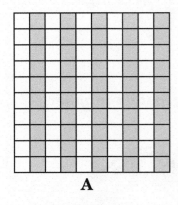

A

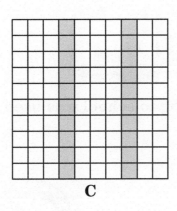

C

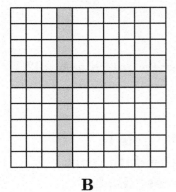

B

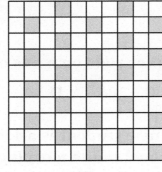

D

Traveling to School

Thirty students were asked how they traveled to school in the morning. Their answers are shown in the tally chart. Study the chart and use it to answer problems 44 through 46.

Bicycle	⊤⊤⊤⊤ ///
Bus	⊤⊤⊤⊤ /
Car	////
Walk	⊤⊤⊤⊤ ⊤⊤⊤⊤ //

44 Which way of traveling to school was used by the greatest number of students?

F bicycle

G bus

H car

J walk

45 How many students either rode on a bus or in a car to get to school?

A 5 **B** 9 **C** 10 **D** 14

46 A new student is asked how she gets to school in the morning. Using the data from the tally chart, which way is least likely to be her answer?

F bicycle

G bus

H car

J walk

47 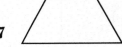 represents 1 unit. Which picture represents one-half unit?

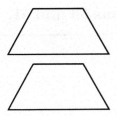

A

B

C

D

48 The picture below shows the first four stages in a pattern of squares.

   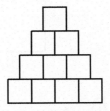

How many squares will there be in the fifth stage?

F   14

G   15

H   16

J   25

49 The figure shown is a cube. Its bottom row contains nine small cubes. How many more small cubes are needed to fill the cube?

A   9 cubes

B   18 cubes

C   27 cubes

D   81 cubes

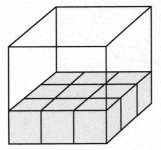

A HIKE IN THE WOODS

Study the map of Sturges State Park. Then answer problems 50 and 51.

50 **How many miles long is the South Road?**

  F   100 miles

  G   80 miles

  H   40 miles

  J   2.5 miles

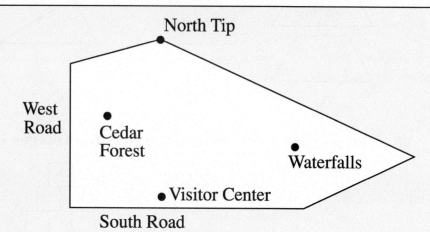

North Tip

West Road

Cedar Forest

Waterfalls

Visitor Center

South Road

Scale
1 inch = 40 miles

51 **A camper wants to hike from the Visitor Center to the Cedar Forest. She estimates that she can walk 3 miles per hour for 7 hours per day. About how many days will it take her to hike to the Cedar Forest?**

  A $\frac{1}{2}$ day

  B   1 day

  C   2 days

  D   3 days

52 A number cube with six sides numbered 1, 2, 3, 4, 5, and 6 is rolled. What is the probability that an odd number will be rolled?

F $\frac{1}{6}$

G $\frac{1}{2}$

H $\frac{9}{12}$

J $\frac{1}{3}$

53 How many *pairs* of congruent shaded figures are there in the grid?

A 1 pair

B 2 pairs

C 3 pairs

D 4 pairs

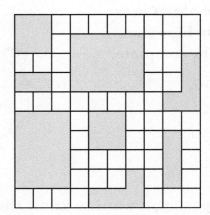

54 Which number sentence fits the diagram?

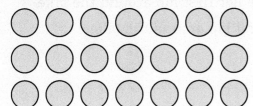

F $7 + 5 \times 3 =$ _____

G $7 + 7 + 7 + 3 =$ _____

H $3 \times 7 \times 5 =$ _____

J $3 \times 7 + 5 =$ _____

Work Out

Ann jogs 12 laps around a lake every evening. It takes her about 45 minutes. Use this information to answer problems 55 and 56.

55 Suppose Ann jogged for 1 hour one night. What would be the most reasonable estimate of how many laps she would complete?

A 16

B 18

C 27

D 13

56 Suppose you want to know the distance around the lake. Which piece of additional information will allow you to find this?

F the amount of time it takes Ann to complete her first lap around the lake

G the average speed at which Ann runs her first lap around the lake

H the total distance Ann jogs each night

J the number of laps Ann completes each week

57 The Bowling Club posted its results from last week's meet. Part of those results is shown.

Member	Scores	Average for the Week
Billy Ru	108, 132, 120	120
Tasha Kittle	116, 88, 105	103
Erica Tandon	93, 132, 111	

What was Erica Tandon's average score last week?

A 109

B 110

C 111

D 112

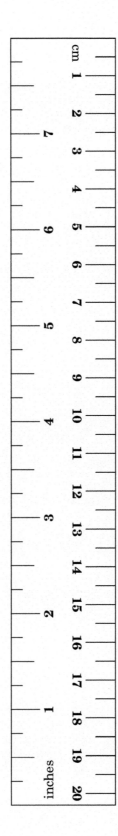

Answer Key

Reading

Lesson 1-p. 7

SA	B	reasons for dancing
SB	G	Amy's mother grew up in San Francisco's Chinatown.
1.	A	boy trying to get the ring on the stick
2.	J	a game called *ajagag*
3.	C	can't play outdoors
4.	G	a bracelet
5.	C	purpose
6.	J	She realized how much work went into it.
7.	C	big enough for a table with four chairs
8.	F	read a book
9.	D	so that he could show her what his father had made
10.	F	insisted
11.	C	They rode the cable down to the ground.
12.	F	excited

Reading Review

Test-p. 12

S	C	hunting buffalo
1.	D	The winner gets a prize.
2.	H	Players must cooperate with one another.
3.	C	in the gym
4.	H	dashing
5.	B	please everybody
6.	H	He let his son ride the donkey.
7.	A	embarrassed
8.	G	to treat badly
9.	B	If you try to please everyone, you will please no one.
10.	F	Jane Addams and Hull House
11.	D	She wanted to become a citizen of the United States.
12.	F	A German immigrant told her about it.
13.	D	She had to learn about the government of the United States.
14.	G	It was a way to make money.
15.	D	merciful
16.	H	Jane Addams was a humanitarian.

Language Arts

Lesson 2-p. 18

SA	B	American Indians were the only people who lived in America until the settlers drove them off their land.
SB	G	He can't dance very well.
1.	A	John grew up blind, but he was determined that it would not hold him back.
2.	H	That day we each made our own kites and flew them in the park.
3.	A	American Indians are the first people who lived in the Americas.
4.	J	They enjoyed themselves at the pow-wow.

Lesson 3-p. 20

SA	D	Next year she's attending the Fashion Institute of Technology.
SB	G	Franklin Delano Roosevelt was paralyzed from polio. However, he still became President of the United States.
1.	A	Then she needs to make sure there will be people who will want to read it.
2.	G	If we know when they are coming, we can be prepared.
3.	B	Because of their great size, people feared the bears. They hunted them in great numbers.
4.	F	These plants, however, were once so prized in Europe, they were transported to North America by the early settlers. Here they were used for food and medicine.

Lesson 4-p. 22

SA	D	It is best as it is.
SB	J	sentence 5
1.	C	My friend and I enjoyed your talk very much.
2.	H	We are both very happy we came.
3.	B	We are hoping to be like you some day.

Test-p. 24

S	C	The rain rolled down the roof.
1.	B	Some of them carry diseases, but they are helpful to nature.
2.	H	They help to make the world a cleaner place to live.
3.	C	When I realized how important insects are, the report took on a different tone.
4.	F	sentence 1
5.	C	after sentence 6
6.	G	He was a 14-year-old soda fountain clerk when he wrote his first piece.
7.	A	He wrote more than a thousand songs.
8.	J	sentence 8
9.	B	He played soft music with mellow tunes and velvety melodies.
10.	J	after sentence 5
11.	A	sentence 1
12.	H	He also played before the Queen of England at her request.
13.	A	Probably no animal has a worse reputation than the wolf.
14.	J	They have a very close family life.
15.	A	The soft, cuddly look of cubs has also made the "teddy bear" a favorite stuffed animal. But if you were to meet a bear in the wilderness, you might not think it was so charming.

Test-p. 29

SA	C	have an enjoyable time
SB	F	The trunk works almost like a hand.
SC	B	after sentence 2
1.	C	a dance that tells a story
2.	G	fun way to learn about history
3.	D	The stories tell about ancestors and events before Kehaulani was born.
4.	J	The dancers spend so much time practicing and performing together.
5.	B	She is radiant in her long dress, called a *mu'u mu'u.*
6.	H	so they only take what they need
7.	D	The ferns are braided.
8.	F	beautiful
9.	D	braid hair
10.	F	Dancing is one of the oldest and liveliest of the arts.
11.	D	It is best as it is.
12.	G	What does dance do for us?
13.	B	It brings people together in thought and feeling.
14.	G	Her movements can tell about religious history and everyday life.
15.	C	The dancer can use any style or form.
16.	J	after sentence 11
17.	D	Today, children enjoy learning to do different tricks with the yo–yo, a toy dating back to ancient times.
18.	H	boy with yo-yo on ground
19.	A	ancient times
20.	H	walking a dog
21.	B	The winner was the contestant who did the most Loop-the-Loops without stopping.
22.	G	come back
23.	B	the information that tells how to return the yo-yo to your hand

24.	G	clever
25.	B	When kids saw the cool tricks, they wanted yo-yos for themselves.
26.	H	Sleeping is a trick anyone can do
27.	D	*The Klutz Yo-Yo Book*
28.	J	Mr. Kane's class visited the library they learned about many games invented in the Philippines and China.
29.	D	World Atlas
30.	H	Games and Recreation in China
31.	A	The child wound the string and held the yo-yo in her palm.
32.	H	Follow these simple instructions.
33.	D	Many children buy game books they learn the rules of different games.
34.	F	she's a girl
35.	B	She says her neck feels cool and free without it.
36.	F	She wants to look and feel more like a boy.
37.	C	Girls almost always wore dresses in those days.
38.	F	determined
39.	B	Sophie could find a girls' baseball team to join.
40.	H	Come see us play the Browning School who beat us last year.
41.	B	We've been practicing all month.
42.	G	Watch us shut out Browning and cheer for our improved team.
43.	D	Baseball Rules
44.	G	hit
45.	C	what grades team members got
46.	H	What are the official rules of the game?
47.	D	It is best as it is.
48.	J	It is best as it is.
49.	C	Is there an opening on the team for me?

50.	H	why there are so many different kinds of snakes on Earth
51.	B	He falls in love with the Moon.
52.	J	delightful
53.	B	The Snake and the Moon get married.
54.	H	The Snake keeps on trying to get the Moon's attention.
55.	C	Remember who and what you are.
56.	J	there is a reason and place for everything in nature
57.	B	The Snake thought the Moon was really in love with him.
58.	G	The snake is often seen as evil. Perhaps we fear the way it slithers so quietly, or maybe we don't like its cold eyes and forked tongue.
59.	C	an ostrich came back to life
60.	G	mild tornado
61.	D	didn't know what makes life begin
62.	J	He took good care of the eggs because they were his children.
63.	A	ostrich feather and the cloud
64.	H	life goes on
65.	C	Although the Biloxi were not afraid, they did not want war.
66.	H	They retreated and built a fort on the edge of a great bay.
67.	D	sentence 10
68.	J	Soon they ran out of food and had to battle another enemy, hunger.
69.	C	after sentence 5
70.	H	sentence 4
71.	A	the tribal name
72.	J	getting along with others
73.	B	it is better to be kind
74.	G	he knows it is his duty
75.	D	gives freely
76.	G	was cruel to her daughter-in-law

77. **B** The mother-in-law was jealous.

78. **F** You will find joy and beauty in your life if you use this towel every day.

79. **C** Another dog also had a bone in its mouth.

80. **G** His bone fell into the water and sank to the bottom.

Mathematics

Lesson 1 - p. 67

S   B
1.   D
2.   G

Lesson 2 - p. 68

S   B
1.   A
2.   H

Lesson 3 - p. 69

S   E
1.   D
2.   F

Lesson 4 - p. 70

S   C
1.   A
2.   G

Lesson 5 - p. 71

S   C
1.   D
2.   H

Lesson 6 - p. 72

S   A
1.   B
2.   H

Lesson 7 - p. 73

S   C
1.   C
2.   G

Lesson 8 - p. 74

S   B
1.   A
2.   G

Lesson 9 - p. 75

S   A
1.   E
2.   J

Mathematics Review

Test - p. 76

S   B
1.   B
2.   K
3.   A
4.   J
5.   B
6.   H
7.   C
8.   G
9.   A
10.   H
11.   B
12.   F
13.   D
14.   G
15.   D
16.   J
17.   A
18.   F
19.   C
20.   H
21.   B

Test - p. 81

SA   B
SB   F
SC   C

Part 1 - p. 83

1.   B
2.   J
3.   D
4.   K
5.   C
6.   F
7.   B
8.   J
9.   C
10.   H
11.   A
12.   G
13.   D

Part 2 - p. 86

14.   J
15.   B
16.   G
17.   B
18.   H
19.   C
20.   J
21.   A
22.   F
23.   D
24.   H
25.   C

26.   G
27.   B
28.   G
29.   A
30.   H
31.   A
32.   G
33.   D
34.   F
35.   C
36.   J
37.   C
38.   G
39.   B
40.   G
41.   A
42.   H
43.   D
44.   J
45.   C
46.   H
47.   D
48.   G
49.   B
50.   F
51.   C
52.   G
53.   C
54.   J
55.   A
56.   H
57.   D

Reading and Language Arts Test Answer Sheet

STUDENT'S NAME

LAST

FIRST

MI

SCHOOL:

TEACHER:

FEMALE ○   MALE ○

BIRTH DATE

MONTH	DAY	YEAR
Jan ○	⓪ ⓪	⓪ ⓪
Feb ○	① ①	① ①
Mar ○	② ②	② ②
Apr ○	③ ③	③ ③
May ○	④	④ ④
Jun ○	⑤	⑤ ⑤
Jul ○	⑥	⑥ ⑥
Aug ○	⑦	⑦ ⑦
Sep ○	⑧	⑧ ⑧
Oct ○	⑨	⑨ ⑨
Nov ○		
Dec ○		

GRADE ③ ④ ⑤ ⑥ ⑦ ⑧

CTB-TerraNova
Reading and Language Arts
Grade 5

The CTB and TerraNova tests are published by CTB McGraw-Hill.
Such company has neither endorsed nor authorized this test-preparation book.

COMPREHENSIVE TEST: Reading and Language Arts

SA Ⓐ Ⓑ Ⓒ Ⓓ
SB Ⓕ Ⓖ Ⓗ Ⓙ
SC Ⓐ Ⓑ Ⓒ Ⓓ

1 Ⓐ Ⓑ Ⓒ Ⓓ
2 Ⓕ Ⓖ Ⓗ Ⓙ
3 Ⓐ Ⓑ Ⓒ Ⓓ
4 Ⓕ Ⓖ Ⓗ Ⓙ
5 Ⓐ Ⓑ Ⓒ Ⓓ
6 Ⓕ Ⓖ Ⓗ Ⓙ
7 Ⓐ Ⓑ Ⓒ Ⓓ
8 Ⓕ Ⓖ Ⓗ Ⓙ
9 Ⓐ Ⓑ Ⓒ Ⓓ
10 Ⓕ Ⓖ Ⓗ Ⓙ
11 Ⓐ Ⓑ Ⓒ Ⓓ
12 Ⓕ Ⓖ Ⓗ Ⓙ
13 Ⓐ Ⓑ Ⓒ Ⓓ

14 Ⓕ Ⓖ Ⓗ Ⓙ
15 Ⓐ Ⓑ Ⓒ Ⓓ
16 Ⓕ Ⓖ Ⓗ Ⓙ
17 Ⓐ Ⓑ Ⓒ Ⓓ
18 Ⓕ Ⓖ Ⓗ Ⓙ
19 Ⓐ Ⓑ Ⓒ Ⓓ
20 Ⓕ Ⓖ Ⓗ Ⓙ
21 Ⓐ Ⓑ Ⓒ Ⓓ
22 Ⓕ Ⓖ Ⓗ Ⓙ
23 Ⓐ Ⓑ Ⓒ Ⓓ
24 Ⓕ Ⓖ Ⓗ Ⓙ
25 Ⓐ Ⓑ Ⓒ Ⓓ
26 Ⓕ Ⓖ Ⓗ Ⓙ
27 Ⓐ Ⓑ Ⓒ Ⓓ
28 Ⓕ Ⓖ Ⓗ Ⓙ
29 Ⓐ Ⓑ Ⓒ Ⓓ

30 Ⓕ Ⓖ Ⓗ Ⓙ
31 Ⓐ Ⓑ Ⓒ Ⓓ
32 Ⓕ Ⓖ Ⓗ Ⓙ
33 Ⓐ Ⓑ Ⓒ Ⓓ
34 Ⓕ Ⓖ Ⓗ Ⓙ
35 Ⓐ Ⓑ Ⓒ Ⓓ
36 Ⓕ Ⓖ Ⓗ Ⓙ
37 Ⓐ Ⓑ Ⓒ Ⓓ
38 Ⓕ Ⓖ Ⓗ Ⓙ
39 Ⓐ Ⓑ Ⓒ Ⓓ
40 Ⓕ Ⓖ Ⓗ Ⓙ
41 Ⓐ Ⓑ Ⓒ Ⓓ
42 Ⓕ Ⓖ Ⓗ Ⓙ
43 Ⓐ Ⓑ Ⓒ Ⓓ
44 Ⓕ Ⓖ Ⓗ Ⓙ
45 Ⓐ Ⓑ Ⓒ Ⓓ

46 Ⓕ Ⓖ Ⓗ Ⓙ
47 Ⓐ Ⓑ Ⓒ Ⓓ
48 Ⓕ Ⓖ Ⓗ Ⓙ
49 Ⓐ Ⓑ Ⓒ Ⓓ
50 Ⓕ Ⓖ Ⓗ Ⓙ
51 Ⓐ Ⓑ Ⓒ Ⓓ
52 Ⓕ Ⓖ Ⓗ Ⓙ
53 Ⓐ Ⓑ Ⓒ Ⓓ
54 Ⓕ Ⓖ Ⓗ Ⓙ
55 Ⓐ Ⓑ Ⓒ Ⓓ
56 Ⓕ Ⓖ Ⓗ Ⓙ
57 Ⓐ Ⓑ Ⓒ Ⓓ
58 Ⓕ Ⓖ Ⓗ Ⓙ
59 Ⓐ Ⓑ Ⓒ Ⓓ
60 Ⓕ Ⓖ Ⓗ Ⓙ
61 Ⓐ Ⓑ Ⓒ Ⓓ

62 Ⓕ Ⓖ Ⓗ Ⓙ
63 Ⓐ Ⓑ Ⓒ Ⓓ
64 Ⓕ Ⓖ Ⓗ Ⓙ
65 Ⓐ Ⓑ Ⓒ Ⓓ
66 Ⓕ Ⓖ Ⓗ Ⓙ
67 Ⓐ Ⓑ Ⓒ Ⓓ
68 Ⓕ Ⓖ Ⓗ Ⓙ
69 Ⓐ Ⓑ Ⓒ Ⓓ
70 Ⓕ Ⓖ Ⓗ Ⓙ
71 Ⓐ Ⓑ Ⓒ Ⓓ

72 Ⓕ Ⓖ Ⓗ Ⓙ
73 Ⓐ Ⓑ Ⓒ Ⓓ
74 Ⓕ Ⓖ Ⓗ Ⓙ
75 Ⓐ Ⓑ Ⓒ Ⓓ
76 Ⓕ Ⓖ Ⓗ Ⓙ
77 Ⓐ Ⓑ Ⓒ Ⓓ
78 Ⓕ Ⓖ Ⓗ Ⓙ
79 Ⓐ Ⓑ Ⓒ Ⓓ
80 Ⓕ Ⓖ Ⓗ Ⓙ

Mathematics Test Answer Sheet

STUDENT'S NAME
LAST   **FIRST**   **MI**

SCHOOL:
TEACHER:
FEMALE ○   MALE ○

(Name grid: columns of bubbles A through Z for each letter position)

BIRTH DATE		
MONTH	**DAY**	**YEAR**
Jan ○	⓪ ⓪	⓪ ⓪
Feb ○	① ①	① ①
Mar ○	② ②	② ②
Apr ○	③ ③	③ ③
May ○	④	④ ④
Jun ○	⑤	⑤ ⑤
Jul ○	⑥	⑥ ⑥
Aug ○	⑦	⑦ ⑦
Sep ○	⑧	⑧ ⑧
Oct ○	⑨	⑨ ⑨
Nov ○		
Dec ○		

GRADE ③ ④ ⑤ ⑥

CTB-TerraNova
Mathematics
Grade 5

The CTB and TerraNova tests are published by CTB McGraw-Hill. Such company has neither endorsed nor authorized this test-preparation book.

COMPREHENSIVE TEST: Mathematics

SA Ⓐ Ⓑ Ⓒ Ⓓ Ⓔ	10 Ⓕ Ⓖ Ⓗ Ⓙ	22 Ⓕ Ⓖ Ⓗ Ⓙ	34 Ⓕ Ⓖ Ⓗ Ⓙ	46 Ⓕ Ⓖ Ⓗ Ⓙ
SB Ⓕ Ⓖ Ⓗ Ⓙ	11 Ⓐ Ⓑ Ⓒ Ⓓ	23 Ⓐ Ⓑ Ⓒ Ⓓ	35 Ⓐ Ⓑ Ⓒ Ⓓ	47 Ⓐ Ⓑ Ⓒ Ⓓ
SC Ⓐ Ⓑ Ⓒ Ⓓ	12 Ⓕ Ⓖ Ⓗ Ⓙ	24 Ⓕ Ⓖ Ⓗ Ⓙ	36 Ⓕ Ⓖ Ⓗ Ⓙ	48 Ⓕ Ⓖ Ⓗ Ⓙ
1 Ⓐ Ⓑ Ⓒ Ⓓ Ⓔ	13 Ⓐ Ⓑ Ⓒ Ⓓ	25 Ⓐ Ⓑ Ⓒ Ⓓ	37 Ⓐ Ⓑ Ⓒ Ⓓ	49 Ⓐ Ⓑ Ⓒ Ⓓ
2 Ⓕ Ⓖ Ⓗ Ⓙ Ⓚ	14 Ⓕ Ⓖ Ⓗ Ⓙ	26 Ⓕ Ⓖ Ⓗ Ⓙ	38 Ⓕ Ⓖ Ⓗ Ⓙ	50 Ⓕ Ⓖ Ⓗ Ⓙ
3 Ⓐ Ⓑ Ⓒ Ⓓ Ⓔ	15 Ⓐ Ⓑ Ⓒ Ⓓ	27 Ⓐ Ⓑ Ⓒ Ⓓ	39 Ⓐ Ⓑ Ⓒ Ⓓ	51 Ⓐ Ⓑ Ⓒ Ⓓ
4 Ⓕ Ⓖ Ⓗ Ⓙ Ⓚ	16 Ⓕ Ⓖ Ⓗ Ⓙ	28 Ⓕ Ⓖ Ⓗ Ⓙ	40 Ⓕ Ⓖ Ⓗ Ⓙ	52 Ⓕ Ⓖ Ⓗ Ⓙ
5 Ⓐ Ⓑ Ⓒ Ⓓ	17 Ⓐ Ⓑ Ⓒ Ⓓ	29 Ⓐ Ⓑ Ⓒ Ⓓ	41 Ⓐ Ⓑ Ⓒ Ⓓ	53 Ⓐ Ⓑ Ⓒ Ⓓ
6 Ⓕ Ⓖ Ⓗ Ⓙ	18 Ⓕ Ⓖ Ⓗ Ⓙ	30 Ⓕ Ⓖ Ⓗ Ⓙ	42 Ⓕ Ⓖ Ⓗ Ⓙ	54 Ⓕ Ⓖ Ⓗ Ⓙ
7 Ⓐ Ⓑ Ⓒ Ⓓ	19 Ⓐ Ⓑ Ⓒ Ⓓ	31 Ⓐ Ⓑ Ⓒ Ⓓ	43 Ⓐ Ⓑ Ⓒ Ⓓ	55 Ⓐ Ⓑ Ⓒ Ⓓ
8 Ⓕ Ⓖ Ⓗ Ⓙ	20 Ⓕ Ⓖ Ⓗ Ⓙ	32 Ⓕ Ⓖ Ⓗ Ⓙ	44 Ⓕ Ⓖ Ⓗ Ⓙ	56 Ⓕ Ⓖ Ⓗ Ⓙ
9 Ⓐ Ⓑ Ⓒ Ⓓ	21 Ⓐ Ⓑ Ⓒ Ⓓ	33 Ⓐ Ⓑ Ⓒ Ⓓ	45 Ⓐ Ⓑ Ⓒ Ⓓ	57 Ⓐ Ⓑ Ⓒ Ⓓ